D1759406

20 14001 868

NEW COLLEGE, SWINDON

To mum and dad, for
your support, every day,
in every way.

Rockport iPad App!
Use your iPad to preview, buy, and read
the latest and greatest from Rockport.

Visit the iTunes App store to download
your free App today!

ROCKPAPERINK

branding • typography • logos • color • design
management • design for change • posters • fashion
www.RockPaperInk.com

© 2012 Rockport Publishers

First published in the United States of America
in 2012 by Rockport Publishers, a member of
Quayside Publishing Group, 100 Cummings
Center, Suite 406-L, Beverly, Massachusetts
01915-6101.
Telephone: (978) 282-9590
Fax: (978) 283-2742
www.rockpub.com

Visit RockPaperInk.com to share your opinions,
creations, and passion for design.

All rights reserved. No part of this book may be
reproduced in any form without written permission
of the copyright owners. All images in this book
have been reproduced with the knowledge and
prior consent of the artists concerned, and no
responsibility is accepted by producer, publisher,
or printer for any infringement of copyright or
otherwise, arising from the contents of this
publication. Every effort has been made to ensure
that credits accurately comply with information
supplied. We apologize for any inaccuracies that
may have occurred and will resolve inaccurate or
missing information in a subsequent reprinting of
the book.

10 9 8 7 6 5 4 3 2 1

ISBN: 978-1-59253-798-3

Digital edition published in 2012.
eISBN: 978-1-61058-423-4

Library of Congress Cataloging-in-Publication
Data is available.

Design: Paul Burgess at Burge Agency,
www.burgeagency.com
Cover Image: Sensus Design Factory Zagreb.
Essays editor: Tony Seddon.

Printed in China

2014001868

Foreword.
Paul Burgess.

For
reword.

Whilst researching for this book, I spent a lot of time contacting different designers from all walks of life: the new kids on the block, the edgy agencies, right through to the forefathers of the industry. One such forefather, or maybe iconic grandfather of design, kindly pointed out to me that he had reached a point in his life where he no longer wanted to contribute to books such as this and had no interest in being published alongside others whose work may not appeal to him.

I hadn't realized it at the time, but my view is quite the opposite. I remember when I first fell in love with design at the age of sixteen, then studying it as a degree, becoming fascinated by type, then to the early days of my career, right though to being a creative director, and even now, running my own agency ... I've always been excited about opening a new book on any design subject, especially one on typography.

You see, I spent those early days looking through books I could only dream to own, being inspired by the great work inside, wishing that one day I might get my work published too. And now, I'm glad to say that (unlike our great forefather), I've reached a point in my life where I'm privileged enough to be able to give some inspiration back through this book.

Whether you're looking upwards with that same youthful, wide-eyed optimism I've always had, or you're an old hand that gets a kick from opening a crisp new tome and seeing a new piece of great typography, I hope this book does it's job of inspiring you.

But whatever happens, don't grow up too much and keep enjoying (and sharing) typography.

Burge.

Conte nts.

Design:Type. An introduction.
Paul Burgess.

n:Type.
oduction.

Design
An intro

"Type? You mean fonts? Like Times New Roman … Oh, no, I like Comic Sans."

For the uninitiated, typography (or fonts to many) is something that, on the whole, passes them by in their every day life. OK, there's the occasional moment of joy in selecting the font for that report or presentation they have to write by Monday or those heady moments of selecting from the default dozen fonts available on their PC to put together a party invite.

But to the initiated, the trained, the experts, and the downright obsessed, typography can become a way of life, and even take it over if you're really lucky.

Simple tasks like reading a book, ordering from a menu, or choosing a birthday card become ordeals. Nice ordeals though. Let's not get down about it. It becomes impossible to read a single word without analyzing the type choice, the way the type's been set, and the context of that type treatment.

But what is good typography? What makes type work? What makes it fail? Why do we get so excited about it?

Anyone who's ever studied fine art, or even gone to a life drawing class, will probably have heard the expression "quality of line," referring to the confidence someone has in putting pen/pencil/brush to paper. A trained eye can see instantly the quality of someone's brush work. The same is true in so many crafts—you could talk about the quality of wine in much the same way. And typography is no different. It's all about the quality—the quality of font, the quality of application, the beautiful balance on the page, and the well-considered hierarchy.

Type is too often "dumped" on a page, with little or no consideration for its real beauty. Rule #1 with typography is to diligently follow all the typographic rules, keep it simple, use a rigid grid structure, never letter-space lowercase text, avoid unbalanced layouts, etc.

Rule #2 is to be empathetic to your audience. Use typography appropriately: Softer, rounder fonts for kids books or toys; harder fonts for corporates; angry fonts for horror movies; serifs for established businesses or classical music.

But aren't rules made to be broken? Absolutely. But to break the rules, you have to know the rules, followed the rules, be an expert in them, and bore people to death with them at dinner parties. Picasso could draw perfectly well (in the traditional sense), but chose not to. If you can't follow the rules, don't break them.

When the rules are followed to the letter (pun intended), beautiful typography can be achieved. When we keep it simple, and appropriate, the results can be stunning. But when we break the rules, we enter a whole other league of design. It's not for the faint-hearted. It takes courage, conviction, and a huge amount of talent—and of course, quality of line— to break the rules and make it work.

For a while now, we've seen this backlash. No sooner had computers become the most valuable design-tool since the lead pencil, than people started to rebel against them. Rule breaking is one thing, but going back to our roots and bringing the pencil alive once again is a completely different way of fighting the rigid type rules. Again, it takes immense skill to make one's own hand-drawn lettering work for a real-world client project. And even more skill to persuade that client it's the right thing to do. But the last decade has given a new lease on life to hand-crafted typography.

Maybe it's the influence of 'new traditionalism' in popular culture, with 1920s and 1950s post-war influences in music and fashion returning to our lives. Or just the resurgence of a values-led societies as the baby-boom Punks and Rockers of the '60s and '70s become grandparents and the more sensitive New Romantics and Goths of the '80s and '90s become parents themselves.

Whatever the influence may be, we are seeing a retro typography comeback, within a contemporary environment. Whether it's the use of serif fonts in a very minimal capacity, or ornate letterforms within funky work, the old-school is definitely back in fashion, and doesn't it look great.

And what about being appropriate and empathetic to our audience? What happens when we use type inappropriately? What happens when we use a serif for a hi-tech product? Or a kid's book? Can we use an angry or raw type treatment to promote the latest romantic-comedy and still make it work? Sometimes making things so wrong can make them right.

We too often create our own boundaries through fear of trying something new. But our boundaries are usually restrained by our clients or the uninitiated who lack the bravery, vision, and skills to think beyond the dozen fonts on their PC.

Invariably, fortune favors the bold, not those that play it safe. So let's all embrace the rules, then let's smash the hell out of them!

Minimal:Type

ESPEJO&
SOMBRAS

Less is much more.

s so n more.

I've spent a lot of my career as a designer, and later as an art director, trying to improve on my editorial layouts for books and brochures by doing less. When I say less, I don't mean I'm not trying so hard—I mean I'm trying to make things simple. This isn't as easy as it sounds, because at the same time, you have to try to make layouts say more. The old adage "Less is More" really rings true here, and I've always felt that the greatest challenge for any designer working with a combination of images and text, or even just text as it goes, is to keep things interesting without sacrificing clarity.

In my opinion, the navigable qualities of any layout are just as important as the quality of the styling or the choice of typeface. It's true to say that it takes skill and practice to select the perfect typeface that completely captures the essence of the project and speaks directly to the readership, but it's a skill that most manage to master to a respectable level. However, I find it astonishing that designers the world over still make so many bad choices in this area. With who knows how many thousands of typefaces to choose from, how can anyone go wrong? The thing is, maybe that huge choice is the root of the problem. It's simply too tempting to say, "Hey, that's a great looking typeface and I'd just love to use it. Let's go for it—I'm in a grungy mood today!" I beg you to stop and consider what you're about to do if you ever have that thought yourself.

The great designer Massimo Vignelli, who has always championed the Modernist tradition for simplicity, is famous for his theory that you only need twelve good typefaces. Search online for "Massimo Vignelli Twelve," and you'll find a fascinating video clip of the man himself explaining why he feels this way. It's interesting stuff, and whilst I have the greatest respect for his work, I cannot agree with him completely as there are far too many exquisite typefaces to limit your collection to only twelve. However, I think he's got a point. I'm straying from the subject slightly, but this is relevant because sometimes the typeface is simply not as important as the way you use it. If you see the typeface first before you understand what the layout is saying to you, you could be on the wrong track.

When it comes to editorial design, the choice of typeface and those navigational properties I mentioned earlier go hand in hand. Typographic hierarchy is one of the greatest assets available to designers wanting to create clear navigation through a layout without having to coax too much effort from the reader. One way to achieve this hierarchy is to use different, and therefore contrasting, typeface families. Another way, a better way if you're striving for simplicity, is to pare down the range of typefaces and use contrasting weights from within a well populated typeface family. Here's a quick tip. Unless you're absolutely sure you won't need them, never choose a typeface for body text that doesn't have at least a roman, semi-bold, and bold weight. Make sure the weights are available in italics too in case you need to emphasize a name or product. Using a coherent set of geometric forms (i.e. the letterforms themselves) from within a single typeface family will make it easier for the reader to scan the text and recognize those forms from one word to the next. Our brain takes snapshots of the character shapes of any one typeface as we read and provides faster feedback when the same characters reoccur. It's a bit like the way computers cache data. And, of course, if you've chosen wisely the layout will look a lot slicker too.

The point I've tried to make here shouldn't be taken universally as sometimes simplicity and clarity isn't what you're after with a layout. There's nothing wrong with slinging a whole bunch of typefaces at a layout if the layout calls for it, and there's nothing wrong with messing about with readability and legibility either if you want to use type illustratively. The most important consideration is one you must make right at the start of a project, before you reach for a pencil or a mouse (and do please consider the pencil option first as good will come of it—I promise you). Learn to think like an editor as well as a designer when working on information-led layouts and make sure that you never have to work hard at trying to decide where your eye should go next. If the story flows effortlessly because of correctly styled text and the smart positioning of all the elements, you've got it right.

Project: Conqueror 3.2
Insert. Art Director:
Nedjeljko Spoljar.
Designers: Nedjeljko
Spoljar, Kristina Spoljar.
Client: ArjoWiggins.

Sensus Design
Factory Zagreb:
Croatia

Project: Conqueror
Stationery Set. Art
Director: Nedjeljko
Spoljar. Designers:
Nedjeljko Spoljar,
Kristina Spoljar. Client:
ArjoWiggins.

Artiva design:
Italy

Artiva design:
Italy

Project: Hello From Artiva Design. Art Directors: Daniele De Batté, Davide Sossi. Designers: Daniele De Batté, Davide Sossi. Client: Artiva Design.

Project: Artiva Business Cards. Art Directors: Daniele De Batté, Davide Sossi. Designers: Daniele De Batté, Davide Sossi. Client: Artiva Design.

DESIGN
DAVIDE SOSSI
VIA GRETO DI CORNIGLIANO 6R (16A)
16152 GENOVA - ITALY
PHONE / FAX: +39 010.86.80.737
MOBILE: +39 338.39.07.119
DAVIDESOSSI@ARTIVA.IT
INFO@ARTIVA.IT
WWW.ARTIVA.IT

ARTIVA DESIGN
DANIELE DE BATTÉ
VIA GRETO DI CORNIGLIANO 6R (16A
16152 GENOVA - ITALY
PHONE / FAX: +39 010.86.80.737
MOBILE: +39 339.63.33.874
DANIELEDEBATTE@ARTIVA.IT
INFO@ARTIVA.IT
WWW.ARTIVA.IT

Artiva design:
Italy

Project: Lettera 22. Art
Directors: Daniele De
Batté, Davide Sossi.
Designers: Daniele De
Batté, Davide Sossi.
Client: Artiva Design.

Lettera22
una ricerca di Emanuele Piccardo su Adriano Olivetti

D14	L22	M1	P101
Divisumma14	Lettera22		
E9000	L32	M20	S42
Elea9000	Lettera32		Studio42
	L80	M40	T
	Lexicon80		Tetractys
		MP1	V
			Valentine

D-Fuse:
UK

Project: Endless Cities.
Art Director: Mike
Faulkner. Designer:
Mike Faulkner.
Client: Mike Faulkner.

9.3 BILLION WORLD POPULATION 2050

75% WILL LIVE IN CITIES IN 2050

8.3 BILLION WORLD POPULATION 2050

64% WILL LIVE IN CITIES IN 2050

1.7 BILLION WORLD POPULATION 1900 10% LIVING IN CITIES IN 1900

6.7 BILLION WORLD POPULATION 2008 50% LIVE IN CITIES TODAY 2008

8.3 BILLION WORLD POPULATION 2050 64% WILL LIVE IN CITIES IN 2050

9.3 BILLION WORLD POPULATION 2050 75% WILL LIVE IN CITIES IN 2050

2030
2 BILLION SQUATTERS

2030
1 IN 4
PEOPLE ON THE PLANET

1.4 MILLION PEOPLE PER WEEK

200 THOUSAND PEOPLE A DAY

130 PEOPLE EVERY MINUTE

MIGRATRAT TO THE CITII

Blok Design:
Canada

Project: *PAR*. Art
Director: Vanessa
Eckstein. Designers:
Vanessa Eckstein,
Patricia Kleeberg.
Client: Moxie Pictures.

FROM 1934 TO 1961, THE PGA OF AMERICA'S "CAUCASIAN-ONLY" CLAUSE WAS A PART OF THE ASSOCIATION'S BY-LAWS AND PREVENTED NON-WHITES FROM MEMBERSHIP. THE CLAUSE WAS REMOVED AT THE 1961 PGA ANNUAL MEETING

THE PGA BROKE MY DAD'S HEART, AS WELL AS A NUMBER OF OTHER GOLFERS WHO SHOULD HAVE HAD AN OPPORTUNITY TO PLAY...THE PGA BROKE THEIR HEARTS AS WELL...

THE REST AREA WAS MY HOTEL

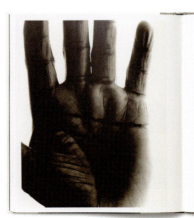

THE PGA OF AMERICA BESTOWED POSTHUMOUS MEMBERSHIP UPON THREE AFRICAN-AMERICAN GOLF PIONEERS —TED RHODES, JOHN SHIPPEN AND BILL SPILLER—WHO WERE DENIED THE OPPORTUNITY TO BECOME PGA MEMBERS DURING THEIR PROFESSIONAL CAREERS. THE PGA ALSO GRANTED POSTHUMOUS HONORARY-MEMBERSHIP TO JOE LOUIS BARROW SR.—BETTER KNOWN AS JOE LOUIS—THE LEGENDARY WORLD HEAVYWEIGHT BOXING CHAMPION WHO BECAME AN ADVOCATE FOR DIVERSITY IN GOLF. THE PGA OF AMERICA BELIEVES THESE MEN, BUT FOR THE COLOR OF THEIR SKIN, WOULD HAVE BEEN PGA MEMBERS WHO PLAY THE GAME, TEACH THE GAME AND PROMOTE THE GAME," SAID PGA OF AMERICA PRESIDENT JIM REMY. "THE PGA OF AMERICA RECOGNIZES THE IMPORTANCE OF HONORING THESE GENTLEMEN WITH THEIR RIGHTFUL PLACE IN GOLF HISTORY."// 2009 FROM PGA AMERICA AT WWW.PGA.COM

A closer look

Blok Design:
Canada

Moxie Films (US) had produced a successful documentary called *Uneven Fairways*, celebrating the African Americans who fought prejudice and segregation for the right to play golf at the highest level. The director wanted to follow this with a book featuring portraits of these legendary golfers by Nike photographer, Michael Faye. Blok developed the title, *PAR*, for its two meanings: the strokes a golfer needs to complete a hole and the struggle to be "on par," or equal. The design is bold, befitting the players, and showcases the intimacy of the portraits.

You'd think that underlining all the text would be anti-minimal, but on such an unaffected page, it adds a striking personality to the text and adds intrigue too.

THE PGA OF AMERICA BESTOWED POSTHUMOUS
SHIP UPON THREE AFRICAN-AMERICAN GOLF PIONEE
—TED RHODES, JOHN SHIPPEN AND BILL SPILLER—WHO
WERE DENIED THE OPPORTUNITY TO BECOME PGA MEM-
BERS DURING THEIR PROFESSIONAL CAREERS. THE PGA
ALSO GRANTED POSTHUMOUS HONORARY-MEMBERSHIP
TO JOE LOUIS BARROW SR—BETTER KNOWN AS JOE LOUIS—
THE LEGENDARY WORLD HEAVYWEIGHT BOXING CHAM-
PION WHO BECAME AN ADVOCATE FOR DIVERSITY IN GOLF.
"THE PGA OF AMERICA BELIEVES THESE MEN, BUT FOR
THE COLOR OF THEIR SKIN, WOULD HAVE BEEN PGA
MEMBERS WHO PLAY THE GAME, TEACH THE GAME AND
PROMOTE THE GAME," SAID PGA OF AMERICA PRESIDENT
JIM REMY. "THE PGA OF AMERICA RECOGNIZES THE IM-
PORTANCE OF HONORING THESE GENTLEMEN WITH THEIR
RIGHTFUL PLACE IN GOLF HISTORY."// 2009 FROM AN ARTICLE AT WWW.PGA.COM

THE PGA BROKE MY DAD'S HEART, AS WELL AS A NUMBER OF OTHER GOLFERS WHO SHOULD HAVE HAD AN OPPORTUNITY TO PLAY...THE PGA BROKE THEIR HEARTS AS WELL...

Simple, beautiful, and effective. The full-bleed text helps change the pace of the book while retaining its minimal approach.

Leaving out the counters in the letters not only makes
die–cutting a lot simpler, but adds a contemporary
edge to the book. It's simple, but effective.

Three letters, one image.
That's a powerful cover.
Blok shows immense
confidence cropping the
image so drastically and
giving the cover so much
breathing space.

Peter Ladd:
Canada

Project: Business Card.
Art Director: Peter Ladd.
Designer: Peter Ladd.
Client: Devin Boquist.

Blok Design:
Canada

**Project: Espejo &
Sombras. Art Director:
Vanessa Eckstein.
Designers: Vanessa
Eckstein, Patricia
Kleeberg. Client:
Fernando Arrioja.**

Blok Design:
Canada

Project: Oueja Negra
Lowe. Art Director:
Vanessa Eckstein.
Designers: Vanessa
Eckstein, Patricia
Kleeberg. Client: Oueja
Negra Lowe.

Artiva Design:
Italy

Project: Lezioni di
Paesaggio #2. Art
Directors: Daniele De
Batté, Davide Sossi.
Designers: Daniele De
Batté, Davide Sossi.
Client: Plug_in edition.

Artiva Design:
Italy

Project: Lezioni di
Paesaggio. Art Directors:
Daniele De Batté, Davide
Sossi. Designers:
Daniele De Batté, Davide
Sossi. Client: Plug_in
edition.

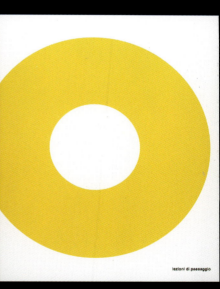

804©:
Germany

Project: Naming booklet.
Art Director: Carsten
Prenger. Designers:
Carsten Prenger, Helge
Rieder, Oliver Henn.
Client: 804© Agentur für
visuelle Kommunikation.

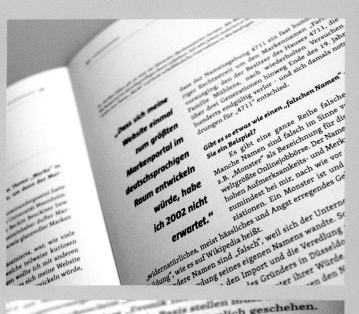

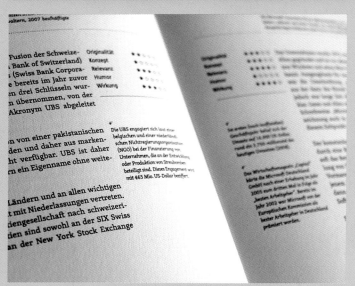

Petralito Rotiroti
Associati:
Italy

Project: *From Z to A,*
a book about Zinc an
Architecture. It's an
upside-down alphabet
to show the application
of Zinc in Architecture all
over the world. Art
Director: Michelangelo
Petralito. Designer:
Iolanda Rotiroti. Client:
VM ZINC, France.

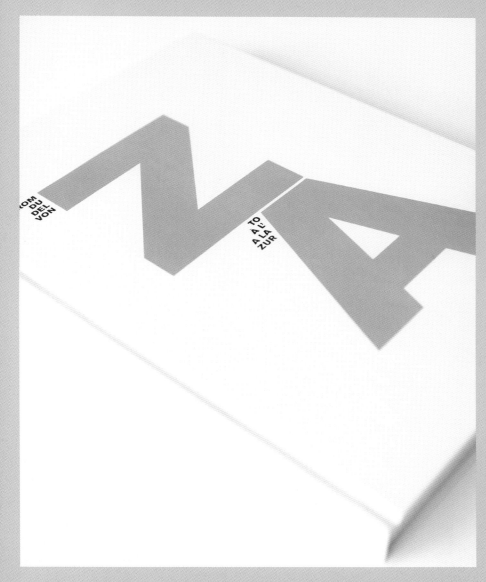

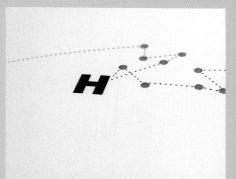

etcorporate design:
Germany

Project: Koepf
Immobilien. Art
Directors: Elisa Huber,
Anton Huber. Designers:
Elisa Huber, Anton
Huber. Client: Koepf
Immobilien.

Aloof:
UK

Project: Business card
and letterhead. Art
Director: Sam Aloof.
Designers: Andrew
Scrace, Jon Hodkinson.
Client: Mclean Quinlan
Architects.

Blok Design:
Canada

Project: *Mexico Ciudad Futura*. Art Director: Vanessa Eckstein. Designers: Vanessa Eckstein, Patricia Kleeberg. Client: Allbero Kalach.

60%
EXTRACCIÓN DEL ACUÍFERO

0%

10%
APROVECHAMIENTO
DE AGUA DE LLUVIA

90

DEL AGUA SE TI
DRENA

10% DEL AGUA SE TRATA Y SE

IENDAS 3.8 millones/**ÁREAS NATURA**

OTEGIDAS 1 319.06km²/**ÁREA DE CUE**

26 km² / **POBLACIÓN** 19 239.910 hab

LIDAD DEL AIRE 80% del año no es satisf

AS VERDES 1.94m² por hab/**ÁREAS**

NADAS 32 000 hectáreas erosionadas/**ÁR**

FORESTADAS 32%del territorio/**RESID**

IDOS 1.17 kilogramos al día por habitante.

Project: Utopia &
Comunità: Antologia.
Art Directors: Daniele De
Batté, Davide Sossi.
Designers: Daniele De
Batté, Davide Sossi.
Client: Plug_in edition.

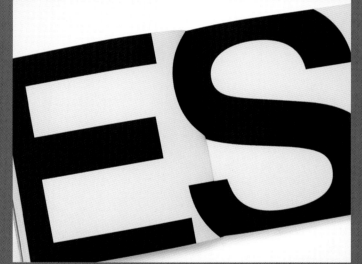

Sensus Design
Factory Zagreb:
Croatia

Project: *First Shot 2010*
Posters. Art Director:
Nedjeljko Spoljar.
Designers: Nedjeljko
Spoljar, Kristina Spoljar.
Client: Galerija Klovicevi
dvori.

A closer look

Sensus Design
Factory Zagreb:
Croatia

Simplicity is beautiful, but simplicity still needs style and even an edge. Type can bring that edge. It's the small details such as the backslashes, odd spacing, and underscores that really bring these posters alive.

These posters for *First Shot 2010*, a photography exhibition series, demonstrate how powerful and successful a series can be. It's always a true test of good typography if it can work across multiple pieces with great effect. The more times the work is rolled out, the more powerful it becomes.

First Shot \2010\
Prvo okidanje

15\09\2010—25\09\2010
FILIP TOT
l.c \   fotografije

Kula Lotrščak \   Zagreb \ ⊛
Strossmayerovo šetalište 9

utorak—petak   17–19h
subota–nedjelja   12–14h

S-6   S-9

First Shot \2010\
Prvo okidanje

\09\2010—25\09\2010
FILIP TOT
l.c\   fotografije

Type layout is like a room in a house—if the room is full of clutter, or is overdesigned, it lacks focus. But a minimal room, with one or two really strong features, can have stunning impact. The cropped numbers give the posters an intriguing focal point, without distracting too much from the photography.

The type is structured, it's rigid, and it fits on a tight grid, but it has a simple, asymmetric twist, giving it a really dynamic feel.

etcorporate design:
Germany

Project: Fair Trade Shop.
Art Directors: Elisa
Huber, Anton Huber.
Designers: Elisa Huber,
Anton Huber. Client: Fair
Trade Shop.

Sensus Design
Factory Zagreb:
Croatia

Project: Curious
Collection Insert.
Art Director: Nedjeljko
Spoljar. Designers:
Nedjeljko Spoljar,
Kristina Spoljar.
Client: ArjoWiggins.

The Room:
Australia

Project: Annual
Report. Art Director:
Andrew Suggit.
Client: Arrow Energy.

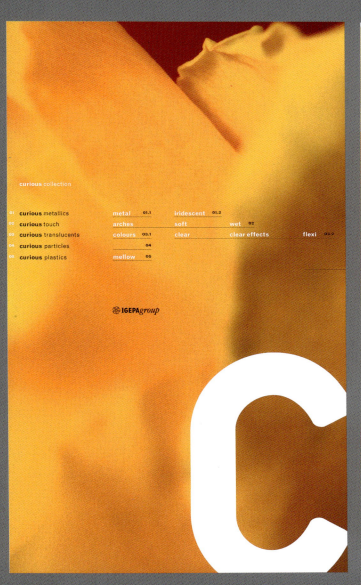

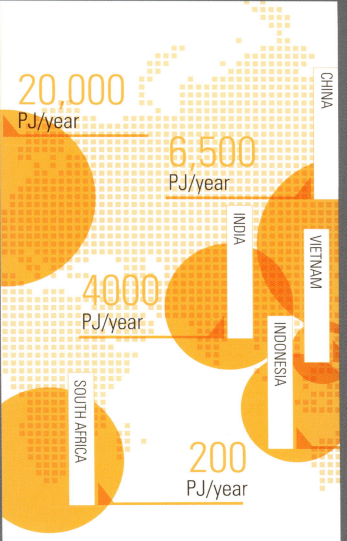

Ken-Tsai Lee Image
Design Company:
Taiwan

Project: The 20 years of
The Prominent Selected
Artists Association of
Taiwan Provincial, Art
Exhibition Group Show.
Designer: Ken-Tsai Lee.
Client: The Prominent
Selected Artists
Association of Taiwan
Provincial.

Ten Gun Design:
USA

Project: Game developer
identity. Designers:
Johann A. Gómez, Ryan
Burlinson. Client: Nuko.

Magma Brand Design:
Germany

Project: *Fonts in Focus 9*.
Art Directors: Flo
Gaertner, Matthias
Kantereit. Client:
Monotype Imaging Ltd,
Linotype GmbH.

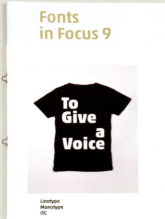

Buddy Carr Skateboards,
The Hello Campaign
www.buddycarrskateboards.com

by Antonio Cavazzini 2010
Typefaces: ITC Avant Garde
www.aventtypedesign.com

Seen

Seen

Fonts in Focus 9

Buddy
Carr
Skateboards

Impressum

A closer look

Magma Brand Design:
Germany

Magma Brand Design recently redesigned Linotype's *Fonts in Focus* publication. It covers interesting and technical aspects from the field of typography, addressing professionals and students in graphic design and typography.

of April 2011.

This very day has also been ... Chahine, who is Linotype's expert wh... are concerned: A great day for her to... newspaper fundamentally consists, ... of text! And it is her typeface designs... plied in the new An-Nahar, some of v... specifically created for the paper's ne... both the artistic and political story a... project on page 2.

No matter if you come from L... from Germany, your own culture, yo... and its own writing system associated... normal and familiar to you. As a resu... about the fact that 'normality' is only a... tive – where typeface is concerned in t... the word! Nowadays, virtually all exist...

PS:
Do you have any questions, suggestions, criticism or praise? Email us: fontsinfocus@linotype.com

Buddy Carr Skateboards,
The Hello Complete
www.buddycarrskateboards.com

by Antonio ...rusone 2010
Typeface: ITC...vant Garde
www.y...fesheep.com

It's a simple trick, but turning type on its side can add intrigue to a minimal layout. It's never popular with clients, but it is a smart wink and a nod to those in the know.

Fonts in Focus 9

Font Playlists

Lamosca, Karlsson Wilker, Jonas Natterer, Kummer & Herrman, Julia Hasting

This page may not be strictly minimal, but it sits within a fairly pure publication and acts a strong pace-changer. What's really nice is the almost accidental nature of the type layout—words overlaying other words and dividing rules out of alignment and cutting through some of the type.

► INDEX

Side – A	Side – B
Helvetica	Futura
Avant Garde	Block Gothic
American Typewriter	Akzidenz Grotesk
New Baskerville	Geogrotesque Stencil
FoundryGridnik	Frankfurter
	Minion

► INDEX

Side – A	Side – B
Trade Gothic, Bold	—
Trade Gothic, Bold No.2	
DIN	
Replica	

► INDEX

Side – A	Side – B
Avenir	Almonte
Giorgio & Giorgio Sans	Neutral BP
Cocksure	URW Globe
Foundry Sterling	Plantin
Albertina	

29

► INDEX

Side – A	Side – B
Akzidenz Grotesk	Neutral
Flama	Replica
Galaxie Polaris	Romain
Haarlemmer	Simple
Hermes	T-Star

► INDEX

Side – A	Side – B
Lettera	Replica
Futura Book	Pica
Akkurat	Walbaum
Arnhem	Joanna
Gravur	

	Side – B
Grotesk	Neutral
Polaris	Replica
...ner	Romain
	Simple
	T-Star

Lamosca
(www.lamosca.com)
is a graphic design studio located
in Barcelona. They work in various
fields of graphic design

karlssonwilker inc.
(www.karlssonwilker.com) got to
be known for their famous work
done for MTV, the MoMA and various
record labels

...Art Director of the famous
mthli German Magazine NEON

Kummer & Herrman
(www.kummer-herrman.nl)
is a famous Utrecht-based Design
Studio with a very strong Direction
in Typography and book making

Julia Hasting
(www.juliahasting.com)
Julia Hasting is a designer and
art director living in Zurich. She is the
creative head of Phaidon Press

Magma Brand Design:
Germany

Project: *ADC Germany Annual 2010*. Art Director: Flo Gaertner. Client: avedition.

Sensus Design
Factory Zagreb:
Croatia

Project: Silvestar Kolbas
Exhibition Catalog.
Art Director: Nedjeljko
Spoljar. Designers:
Nedjeljko Spoljar,
Kristina Spoljar. Client:
Galerija Klovicevi dvori.

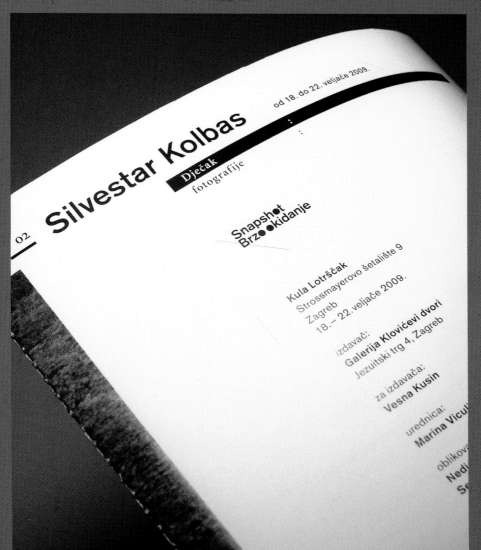

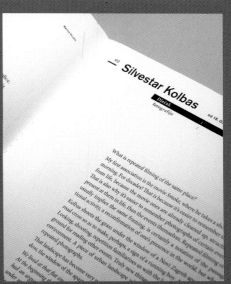

Sensus Design
Factory Zagreb:
Croatia

Project: Conqueror
Catalog 3.0. Art Director:
Nedjeljko Spoljar.
Designers: Nedjeljko
Spoljar, Kristina Spoljar.
Client: ArjoWiggins.

The Allotment:
UK

Project: White Logistics
& Storage. Art Directors:
James Backhurst,
Michael Smith, Paula
Talford, Paul Middlebrook.
Designers: James
Backhurst, Michael
Smith, Paula Talford,
Paul Middlebrook.
Client: White Logistics
& Storage.

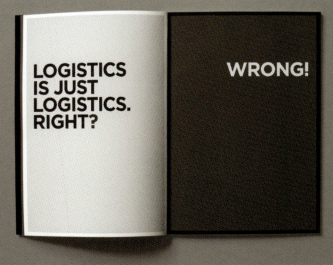

Curious:
UK

Project: BTMK. Art
Director: Peter Rae.
Designer: Louise
Desborough. Client:
BTMK.

Project: Ai Wei Wei.
Art Director: Rose.
Designer: Rose.
Client: Tate Modern.

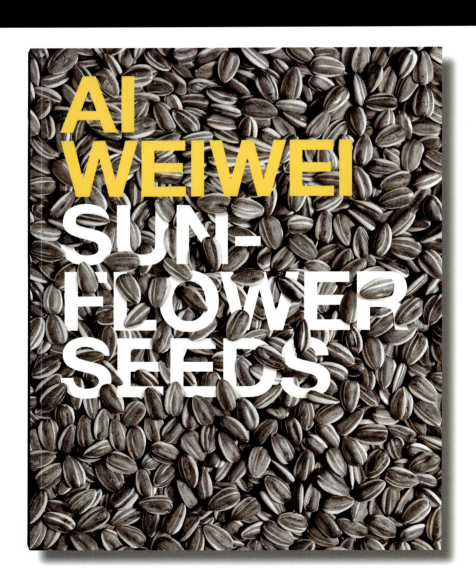

Michael Lashford Design:
USA

Project: Cactus Cantina logo, for a Mexican restaurant and bar. Art Director: Michael Lashford. Client: Cactus Cantina.

One Man's Studio:
USA

Project: Article 25 Logo, created for a human rights newspaper. Art Director: Keith Kitz. Designer: Keith Kitz. Client: Article 25.

Bruketa & Žinić:
Croatia

Project: MC redesign. Creative Directors: Miran Tomičić, Davor Bruketa, Nikola Žinić. Art Director: Miran Tomičić. Designer: Tanja Pružek Šimpović. Client: TDR.

Project: Semplici
Architetture. Art
Directors: Daniele De
Batté, Davide Sossi.
Designers: Daniele De
Batté, Davide Sossi.
Client: Artiva Design.

Artiva Design:
Italy

Project: P. Soleri DVD
38'38". Art Directors:
Daniele De Batté, Davide
Sossi. Designers:
Daniele De Batté, Davide
Sossi. Client: Plug_in
edition.

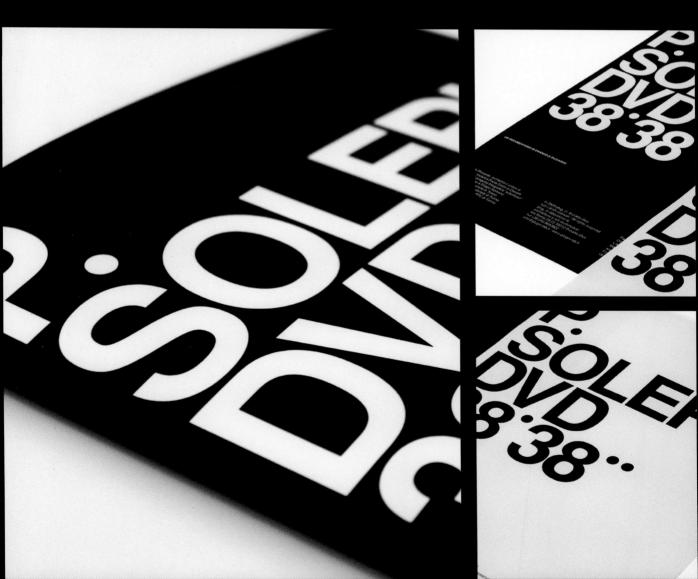

Sensus Design
Factory Zagreb:
Croatia

Project: Gerila Media,
visual identity. Art
Director: Nedjeljko
Spoljar. Designers:
Nedjeljko Spoljar,
Kristina Spoljar.
Client: Gerila Media.

Project: Òptic.
Art Director: Dorian.
Designer: Dorian.
Client: Òptic.

Dorian:
Spain

Project: Takto.
Art Director: Dorian.
Designer: Dorian.
Client: Takto Jewellery
Design.

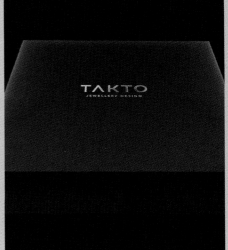

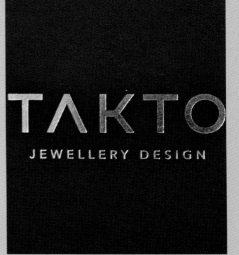

Sensus Design
Factory Zagren:
Croatia

Project: Metronet Sales
Brochure. Art Director:
Nedjeljko Spoljar.
Designers: Nedjeljko
Spoljar, Kristina Spoljar.
Client: Metronet
Telecommunications.

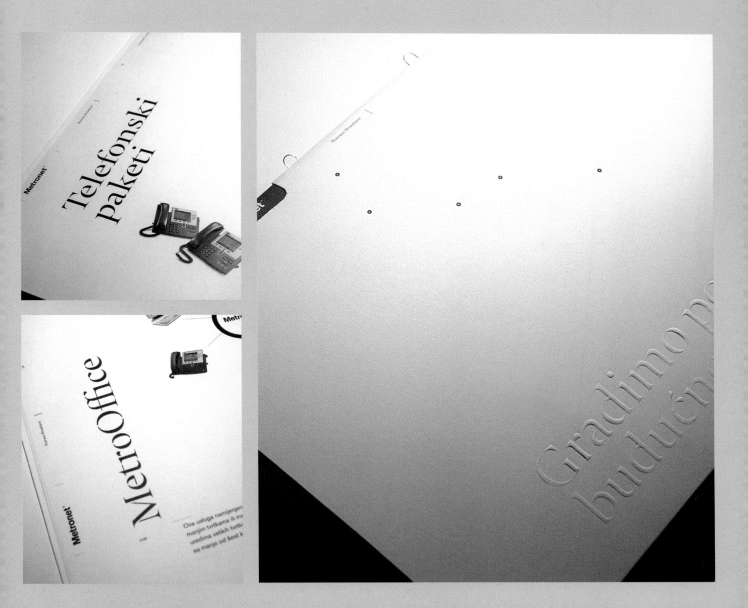

Project: *Textual
Moments* book series.
Designer: Paul Burgess.
Client: Bloomsbury
Academic.

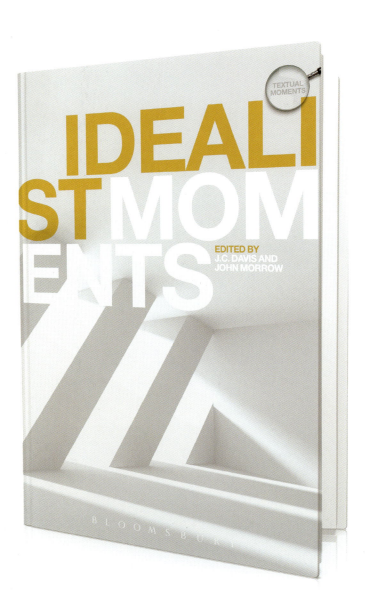

Project: Manifesta.
Client: Manifesta 9.

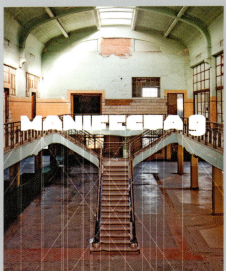

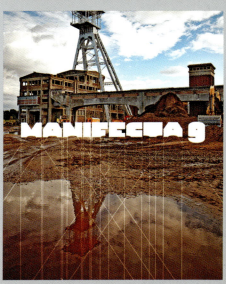

Burge Agency:
UK

Project: Gauge.
Designer: Paul Burgess.
Client: Gauge 360
software.

Project: Dyneema
D12 branding. Designer:
Paul Burgess. Client:
English Braids.

Project: Inca branding.
Designer: Paul Burgess.
Client: Twinings.

Project: South One
Media branding.
Designer: Paul Burgess.
Client: South One Media.

Artiva Design:
Italy

Project: Energy
Company logo and
corporate identity. Art
Directors: Daniele De
Batté, Davide Sossi.
Designers: Daniele De
Batté, Davide Sossi.
Client: Energy Company.

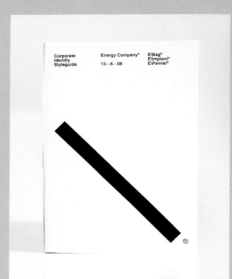

Artiva Design:
Italy

Project: Dopo la
rivoluzione. Art Directors:
Daniele De Batté, Davide
Sossi. Designers: Daniele
De Batté, Davide Sossi.
Client: Plug_in edition.

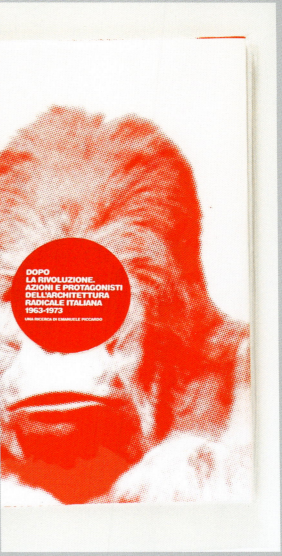

DOPO
LA RIVOLUZIONE.
AZIONI E PROTAGONISTI
DELL'ARCHITETTURA
RADICALE ITALIANA
1963-1973
UNA RICERCA DI EMANUELE PICCARDO

Project: Metal brand
Identity. Art Director: Ian
Thompson. Designer:
Richard Bassett. Client:
Metal Culture.

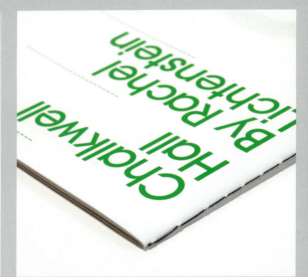

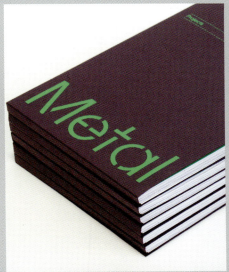

Artiva Design:
Italy

Project: Due Zero Uno
Zero. Art Directors:
Daniele De Batté, Davide
Sossi. Designers:
Daniele De Batté, Davide
Sossi. Client: Plug_in
edition.

Foreign Policy
Design Group:
Singapore

Project: The Waterhouse
at South Bund, Shanghai.
Art Director: Yah-Leng Yu.
Client: The Waterhouse at
South Bund, Shanghai.

Ragged:Type

work
Info

ADLtd. Branding & Visual Style

Brand restyling and art direction of cover style for american techno label ADLtd, run by swedish Dj and producer Alexi Delano.

IMAGE **2/8**

Back

Jose Palma

all works © Jose Palma. 2006 · 2011

Breaking the rules:
Jorge Restrepo

Breaki the **ng e rules.**

It is in some ways difficult to talk about typography when you create it the way I do.

Some time ago, tired of the work I was making using my computer, I decided to leave behind all the things that tied me to my desk—clients, administration, and accounts—all of the everyday tasks I was used to. I knew this was risky, but it was necessary. The idea was that once the decision was made, I could relax and breathe new life into my work. It wasn't long—just a few weeks really—before I wanted to begin working again, but I was not going back to my computer and my old clients. I decided to look for new beginnings with a pencil and paper and went back to school.

Faced with a blank sheet of paper, it was clear that I needed to learn to work in new ways, so I turned to a technique that I had always wanted to explore more thoroughly—collage. Searching for points of reference, I found many of them in the art of Rauschenberg, Warhol, and others. I learned the technique of cut and paste. However, something was missing, so I began to introduce typography to the equation. This typography was not created on a computer, but by using hand lettering—a difficult technique to get right.

I am not about to give you a lesson in how to do hand lettering. I believe strongly that the best approach to hand lettering is a personal approach, where you achieve the results through your own aesthetic and style. Instead, I would like to discuss the process I put together for each of my projects, remembering that the collage technique provides me with the motivation for drawing letters. My technique is all about deconstruction—every new collage I start provides me with the ideal way of creating new letterforms. I start by taking existing typographic forms, and then I mix everything together, adding and taking away, until I create what I call "Frankenstein typography." Every new project produces something different, and sometimes I will create a complete new alphabet, but other projects I only create a single word or sentence.

I might take the stem of a Garamond A, a serif of an art deco alphabet sourced from an old magazine my Grandmother gave me, a swash from the typography found on a favorite vintage poster, or an arm from an antique postcard for the Mercado de las Puglas restaurant in Mexico. Mix all of these elements together and you have everything you need to create a beautiful new character.

It is a difficult process mainly because there are no guidelines to follow. There is no sketch or plan so you never know quite where the process will end or what your finished type will look like. However, this is what makes the process so exciting. Without a plan, the mistakes and the randomness provide you with your best design tools. I always try to go with the process, without going back over a letterform to make another attempt at forming it. I also try to use lots of different paper stocks and surfaces such as kraft paper, watercolor, and canvas and use a wide variety of tools including brushes, colored pencils, pens, and markers. The right letterforms for each of my projects result directly from the experimental process.

The letters have to be drawn with confidence directly onto the collaged composition, so you cannot be afraid to make the marks. It can be a risky procedure, but if you experiment first you will in most cases get the results you were expecting. I do not mind admitting that some pieces have been ruined during construction by the bad execution of a letterform or spilled and splattered ink, but I do not think of this as a problem. It is my job.

The process can be very time-consuming too, as in the case of 1970, which is a biographical piece, a self-portrait if you like. All the separate items of text carry some context with events in my life. It took a month to complete, with about twenty days spent on the typography. I used charcoal on watercolor paper—not recommended—but it allowed me to create the exact feeling I wanted for the piece, something a little chaotic.

The key to everything for me is to deconstruct. Whether a piece is analog or digital, a personal piece or something that has been commissioned, everything is constructed from deconstruction.

Wonksite Studio:
Colombia

Project: Dejando Huella.
Art Director: Jorge
Restrepo. Designer:
Jorge Restrepo. Client:
Tipos Libres.

Viviana Gomez:
Colombia

Project: Cups. Art
Director: Viviana Gomez.
Designer: Viviana
Gomez. Client:
Illustrated.

Wonksite Studio:
Colombia

Project: Self promo
posters/workshop.
Art Director: Jorge
Restrepo. Designer:
Jorge Restrepo. Client:
Tipos Libres.

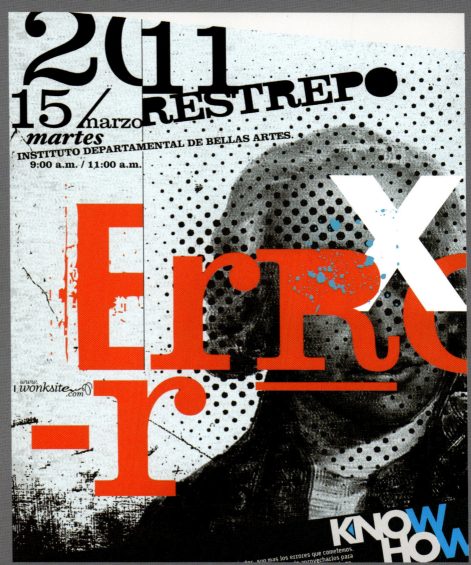

Magma Brand Design:
Germany

Project: *Fresh – Cutting Edge Illustrations*. Art Directors: Lars Harmsen, Philipp Louven. Client: daab Media.

— Make a statement

Interview with Pure Evil

In 1990 PURE EVIL left the P... behind and went to live in Cali... years ingesting weapons-grade... about stuff, making electronic m... Inspired by skateboard cultur... character graffiti of Twist he... picked up a spraycan and starte... vampire bunnies everywhere.

You opened the *Pure Evil Galle...* heart of Hoxton, London. Wha... street art and graffiti-influence...

I had worked on a Santas Gh... my own space. Santas Ghetto wa... and Co. took over an old shop an... was a lot of fun. I decided to do so... also based on Aaron Rose's ALL... New York in the 90s. It was a... way to ease into running a galler...

Are there certain pieces that y... show in the gallery space rath...

No I don't think so, maybe... completely HUGE that wouldn't...

10

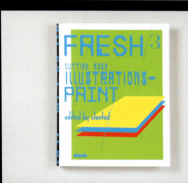

D-Fuse:
UK

Project: Sony-E-Reader
film for installation.
Art Director: Mike
Faulkner. Designer:
Paul Mumford. Client:
Sony/Fallon.

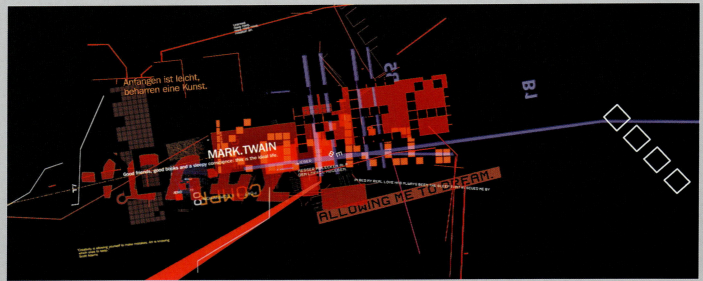

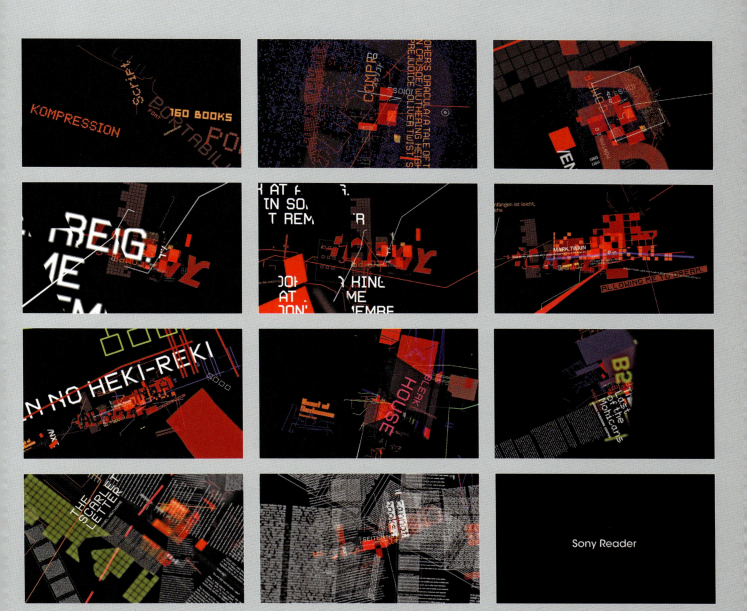

Magma Brand Design:
Germany

Project: *Fake or Feint*.
Art Director: Flo Gaertner.
Client: agrobooks.

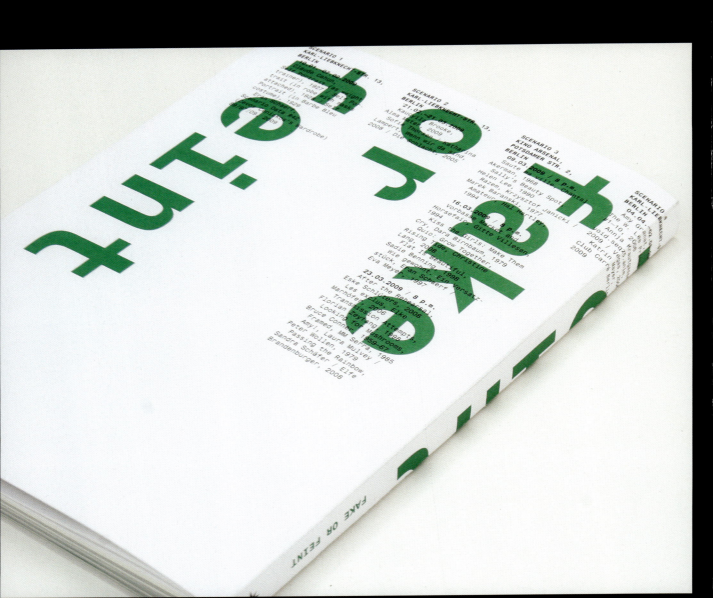

tarting
nclude
oping the
ng a
inars,
tions
ar
in
r
es

Scenario

The first s
Cahun togeth
of earlier w
common is the
staging and co
ited: Self Portrait (in robe
made in 1928, an
from 1929. E
portraits. Alwa

Self Portrait

Three of Claude

(Devos Canakos's Wardrobe)
89/97/09/ 2009
Scenario Data #42,
Erna Schaert
costume), 1929
Portrait (in Barbe Bleu
attached), 1928 /Self
trait (in robe with masks
trainer), 1927 /Self Por
Claude Cahun,
Self Portrait (as naught

2008 / Die Sab
Lampert; Wenn
Alma Mater
Kaouc
BERL

Brunnerweg, 2008
Sandra Gamix / ETTO
PASSING the balloon,
Anni, Laura Walter,
Bruce Connor, 1965
Looking, NW space, 1985
Florian Morlat
Translocation
Wardrobe1, 2008
Los exyam, 1985
After the Burning
Eska Sonlum, 2008
23.03.2009 / 8 p.m.
Eva Meyer, 1987
stock, the Situ
Rising, 2008
Lang, 20
flat is
Sadie Benni
cry
outsta

Jillian Coorey:
USA

Project: Poster for Perrin
Stamatis exhibition.
Designer: Jillian Coorey.
Client: Perrin Stamatis.

Jimmy Ball
Design:
USA

Project: Trading Card
graphic for AIGA Dallas
Fort Worth. Art Director:
Jimmy Ball. Client: AIGA
Dallas Fort Worth.

Perrin Stamatis
The Love Song of J. Alfred Prufrock

The Art Institute of Chicago
111 South Michigan Ave
Chicago, Illinois / June 5–July 26 2011

Bruketa & Žinić:
Croatia

Project: Everyday Design.
Creative Directors: Davor
Bruketa, Nikola Žinić. Art
Directors, Designers:
Imelda Ramović, Mirel
Hadžijusufović. Client:
Proposal.

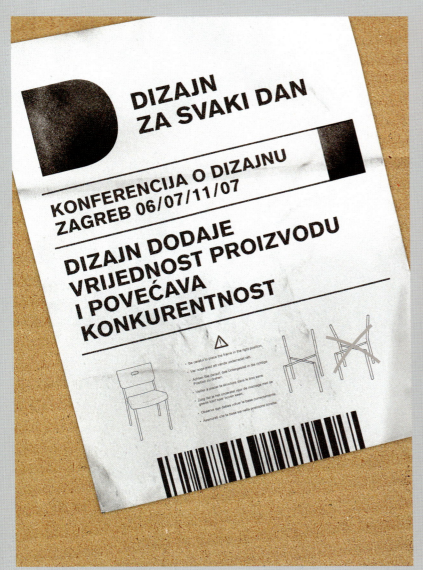

LSDspace:
Spain

Project: VIHvo font.
Art Directors: Gabriel
Martínez, Manuel
Ponce. Designers:
Gabriel Martínez,
Manuel Ponce. Client:
VIHvo festival 2010.

LSDspace:
Spain

Project: book and type
illustrations. Art
Directors: Sonia Díaz,
Gabriel Martínez.
Designer: Gabriel
Martínez. Client:
ADACYL/MUSAC.

Wonksite Studio:
Colombia

Project: Stats. Art
Director: Jorge
Restrepo. Designer:
Jorge Restrepo. Client:
mySHELF project.

A closer look

Wonksite Studio:
Colombia

Wonksite Studio was commissioned to create a wallpaper background for a design studio. The most interesting and adaptable solution was a typographic treatment that personifies the designers and their interests.

+ WONKSITE STUDIO + Copyright © Jorge Restrepo 2009. All rights reserved. No part of this design shall produced, stored in a retrieval system, or transmitted by any means – electronic, mechanical, photocopying, ing, or otherwise – without written permission from the author. No patent liability is assumed with respect to of the information contained herein. Although every precaution has been taken in the preparation of this des author assume no responsibility for errors or omissions. Neither is any liability assumed for damages resulti the use of the information contained herein.

Type gone mad? At first glance it may look like a keyboard has exploded across this shelf, but actually this is superbly organized and information design at its very best.

Every element of type detail is considered on a micro and macro level. Close up, it has fascinating detail, and from afar, it creates a stunning texture.

The range of typefaces looks extensive, but in fact there aren't as many as it may seem. Instead scale, rotation, weights, and layout help give the piece a very ragged, busy, and maximalist feel.

Un Mundo Feliz:
Spain

Project: fanzine *BOLD*.
Art Directors: Sonia Díaz,
Gabriel Martínez.
Designer: Gabriel
Martínez. Client: DA2
contemporary art center.

BOLD

Bold Fanzine #2
Primavera / verano 2009
Special DA2 Issue

el secreto
de la felicidad

"Aviso a los
padres:
contenido explícit-
o"

___Bold_ 4/5

Los periódicos y la televisión nos dan una imagen brutal
y violenta de la realidad: conflictos armados, tornados,
terremotos, asesinatos, accidentes de todo tipo, crisis
económicas, etc. Esta distorsión de la verdad se basa
según Dale Carmegie en el encuadre de los mass media,
pues "aproximadamente el noventa por ciento de las
cosas de la vida están bien y el diez por ciento mal".
"Teniendo en cuenta el nivel de población alcanzado y
lo abarrotado que actualmente está el planeta, somos en
realidad una especie increíblemente pacífica y amable.
Quien abrigue dudas, que pruebe a contar los miles de
millones de seres humanos que se han levantado esta
mañana y han pasado la jornada sin darse de puñetazos.

Las malas
noticias
son las auténticas
noticias
!"$=?_-

___Bold_ 2/3

editorial:

la vida es
una desgracia con-
tinua
interrumpida
por breves mo—
mentos
de felicidad

SOBRE LOS MECANISMOS INVISIBLES

MUNTADAS ABOUT INVISIBLE MECHANISMS

[MUNTADAS] PERSONAL / PUBLIC INFORMATION
VANCOVER ART GALLERY 1979]

"El hombre es un animal agresivo. A excepción de ciertos roedores, ningún vertebrado actúa de modo tan sistemático y frenético a miembros de su propia especie. Hemos definido la psicología social como influencia social —esto es, como influencia de una persona (o grupo) sobre otra persona (o grupo)—. La forma más extrema de agresión (la destrucción física) puede considerarse como el último grado de la influencia social." (Elliot Aronson, La agresividad humana)

PINTA, COLOREA O HAZ LO QUE QUIERAS (#6)
GENTE SWOOSH
COLECCIÓN "PROBANDO MI ARMA"

play

JUST TESTING MY GUN ★ SWOOSH PEOPLE

Manipulación, propaganda
y democracia
en Un mundo feliz

SH **LA CULTURA DEL MERCADO ES LA CULTURA DE LA EXCLUSIÓN. AQUÍ SÓLO VALEN LOS MÁS FUERTES, RICOS Y FAMOSOS.**

"Una chica deja de comer para lograr esa absurda delgadez de las modelos. Otra se suicida porque no logra dejar de verse gorda. Un muchacho roba para poder comprar la droga que, a su vez, le permitirá sentirse parte de un grupo. Otro se suicida porque sabe que sus notas en el colegio van a enfurecer a sus padres. Una niña se prostituye porque no llega dinero a su casa, lo va a pasar mal. Otra se fuga de su hogar para intentar salvarse de los abusos y los malos tratos cotidianos. Un adolescente se deprime porque no logra alcanzar el primer puesto en alguna competición deportiva. Otro sufre las burlas cotidianas, a raíz de alguna discapacidad que lo diferencia.

Estos personajes viven en distintos lugares, pertenecen a distintos sectores socioeconómicos, pero hay algo que los une: se sienten presionados/as creen que si no cumplen con determinados requerimientos serán rechazados/as, no podrán satisfacer las expectativas de los demás." (Cont. Jorge y Peyró, Graciela María, 2003)

Bold 10/11

[U&? Nero Noise Brasil (206)
Goudom (Segado & autómatas FIER)]

Bold _ 16/17

TODAS LAS ACTIVIDADES ARTÍSTICAS SE HAN APOYADO EN SISTEMAS DE REPRESENTACIÓN QUE TRATAN DE DAR FORMA VISIBLE A LOS DIVERSOS DISCURSOS O PERCEPCIONES PERSONALES. ENTRE ESTOS SISTEMAS SE ENCUENTRAN EL DIBUJO, LA PINTURA, LA ESCULTURA, ETC. EL ESPECTRO DE LOS TEMAS REPRESENTADOS POR ESTOS SISTEMAS VARÍA ENTRE LA REPRESENTACIÓN DE LA REALIDAD Y LA REPRESENTACIÓN DEL FENÓMENO DE IRREALIDAD; ENTRE LA DURA REALIDAD Y LA FICCIÓN MÍTICA, ENTRE EL PANFLETO POLÍTICO Y LA ALUCINACIÓN. A ESTOS SISTEMAS Y TÉCNICAS TRADICIONALES DE VISUALIZACIÓN, SE HAN UNIDO OTROS SISTEMAS QUE HAN IDO SURGIENDO DE RECIENTES DESARROLLOS TÉCNICOS EN LA ESFERA DE LOS MEDIA. LOS MEDIA, QUE NACEN COMO PORTADORES NEUTRALES DE PURO DISCURSO, SE VEN MANIPULADOS POR SISTEMAS INVISIBLES.

DENTRO DEL CONTEXTO DE LA LUCHA POLÍTICA ACTUAL, TANTO LOS GRUPOS DOMINANTES COMO LOS DE OPOSICIÓN ARTICULAN Y DISEMINAN LA INFORMACIÓN A TRAVÉS DE LA ACEPTACIÓN Y MANIPULACIÓN DE ESTOS "MECANISMOS INVISIBLES". LA RETENCIÓN DEL PODER DEPENDE DE LA "SEDUCCIÓN DE LAS MASAS". LAS DISTINTAS ESTRATEGIAS DE MEDIOS, LAS TÉCNICAS SUBLIMINALES, ETC., SON "EL PERFUME Y LAS FLORES" UTILIZADOS PARA ESTA SEDUCCIÓN.

A TRAVÉS DE CAMPAÑAS, CARTELES, RADIO Y TELEVISIÓN, EL PODER SE IMPONE; NO POR LAS ARMAS, SINO MÁS BIEN POR EL SONIDO Y LA IMAGEN.

LA MANERA EN QUE LEEMOS ESTA INFORMACIÓN Y HASTA QUÉ PUNTO SOMOS CONSCIENTES DE SU PODER PERSUASIVO, TIENE QUE VER CON NUESTRO TRATAMIENTO SUBJETIVO Y OBJETIVO DE LA INFORMACIÓN, A MEDIDA QUE NOS ENFRENTAMOS CON ELLA. LA NATURALEZA Y VOLUMEN DE LA TRANSMISIÓN, ASÍ COMO EL DE NUESTRA RECEPCIÓN, JUNTO CON NUESTRAS CONCEPCIONES CULTURALES, HISTÓRICAS Y ESPACIOTEMPORALES, AFECTAN NUESTRA DEFINICIÓN DEL CARÁCTER DEL MENSAJE.

Wonksite Studio:
Colombia

Project: Self promo posters/workshop.
Art Director: Jorge Restrepo. Designer: Jorge Restrepo. Client: Wonksite Studio.

Alex Trochut:
Spain

Project: Neo Deco. Art Director: Alex Trochut. Client: Huge for Type.

ILLUSTRATION VOLUME ET 3D

Wonksite Studio:
Colombia

Project: Self promo
posters/workshop.
Art Director: Jorge
Restrepo. Designer:
Jorge Restrepo. Client:
Wonksite Studio.

WONKSITE ESTUDIO
PRESENTA

NO
LE TENGO
MIEDO
A LA
TIPO
GRA
FIA.

EN GUAYAQUIL
(EN HUESO Y CON CARNE)

Jorge Restrepo es diseñador gráfico graduado con honores de la Universidad Nacional de Colombia en el 2001, también es Adobe Certified Expert. Ha trabajado como Director de Arte para Revista Cambio e Inter-Cambio, trabajó como Director de Arte en JWT, y es profesor del departamento de diseño en la Universidad de Los Andes. Paralelamente, desde hace 10 años tiene su propio estudio de diseño « WONKSITE STUDIO +. En el 2010 crea la editorial [ing.] editores que se lanza con el libro: [fing.] 50 FORMAS DE VER LA ILUSTRACIÓN. Ha desarrollado proyectos como I love Haiti junto a Pechakucha Night (2010) y en el 2008 fue curador de la exposición en Hong Kong titulada Colombia Passion. Es coautor del libro Masters of Photoshop Volume 2, y participado en libros como LatinAmerican Graphic Design (TASCHEN), Atlas of Graphic Design (Max Máci), ¿What do you love? (109, China 2010), 1000 type treatments (Rotovision), Dolce & Gabbana Aniversary Book, NLF Book (Musa), Latinamerican design (Zeixs), entre otros.

TALLER / 3 MÓDULOS
1. Collage
La importancia de cortar y pegar en el diseño y
como aplicarlo a la gráfica.
2. Typo Experimental
Las letras no solamente sirven para comunicar,
a veces tienen un valor estético.
3. Objeto (collage + typo)
Integrar formas que lleven significado a partir
de la deconstrucción.

-FECHA-
18 y 19 de abril del 2011
-LUGAR-
Facultad de Arquitectura y Diseño de la UCSG
-HORARIO-
9h00 a 14h00 horas
-ACREDITACIÓN-
2 créditos, previa presentación de trabajo y el pago de la inscripción.
-VALOR-
$180
-INSCRIPCIONES-
En secretaría de la Facultad de Arquitectura y Diseño UCSG
-INFORMACIÓN-
Contactarse a través del correo electrónico de la Asociación de Estudiantes de Arquitectura y
Diseño aefa.ucsg@gmail.com o en la secretaría de la Facultad.

UNIVERSIDAD CATÓLICA
DE SANTIAGO DE GUAYAQUIL

sparc, inc:
USA

Stephan Walter:
Switzerland

Vamadesign:
Greece

Project: Event branding
and communications for
DIFFA's annual gala. Art
Director: Richard Cassis.
Designer: Richard
Cassis. Client: DIFFA
(Design Industries
Foundation Fighting
AIDS) Chicago.

Project: Gig poster for
band *One of the Kind*.
Designer: Stephan
Walter. Client: El Lokal.

Project: *Edward
Scissorhands*
redesigned movie
poster. Art Director:
Vasilis Magoulas.
Designer: Vasilis
Magoulas. Client:
Self-promotion.

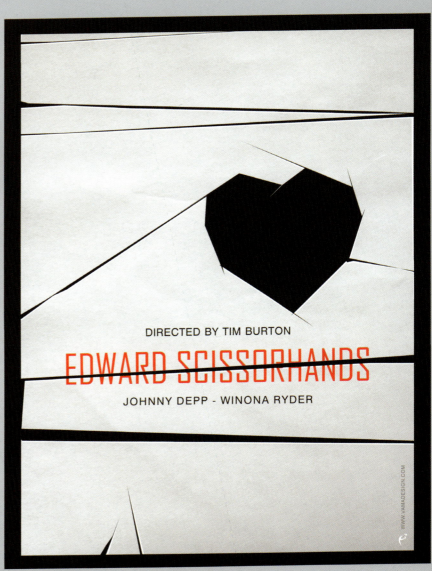

Marshall Rake:
USA

Project: Identity design for modern café, in Los Angeles. Designer: Marshall Rake. Client: Paper or Plastik Café.

Uretsky & Co:
USA

Project: Logo for a production of play "God of Carnage". Art Director: Jan Audun Uretsky. Designer: Jan Audun Uretsky. Client: Mile Square Theatre.

Juicebox Designs:
USA

Project: Book about growing closer to God, Jump: Into a Life of Further and Higher. Art Directors: Jay Smith, Amy Kiechlin. Designer: Jay Smith. Client: David C Cook.

PAPER OR PLASTIK CAFE

GOD OF CARNAGE
A COMEDY OF BAD MANNERS

The woman on staff at the zoo told some interesting facts to Darrell and his son about the Impala. She said that the African Impala has the ability to jump 13 feet high in the air from the position of standing still. This allows the Impala to escape predators that try to sneak up on it from behind. When on the move the Impala has the ability to not only jump 13 feet high, but also jump 30 feet out. The back of the Impala is like a shock absorber that gives it the ability to leap high. This leap is like an explosion. Impalas can also reach maximum running speeds of close to 60 miles per hour. Again, this natural ability of the Impala is what makes it possible to escape other animals that maybe trying to attack. But then she went on in her presentation to bring up something else that really caught Darrell's attention. "Notice that even though the Impala has the ability to jump 13 feet high and 30 feet out that the African Impala's are initially contained here at the Zoo by a 3-foot wall!" As Darrell was telling me this story I had to stop him right there.

How is it that the African Impala has the ability to jump 13 feet high and 30 feet out but can be initially contained by a 3-foot wall? This right here shows my tendency just to get distracted in a conversation but also talk too much and not listen very well. Thank God for Darrell understanding this struggle I have. He went on to say that the staff person from the Zoo explained that when the African Impala's are young they teach them that they can't jump over the 3-foot wall. They do this by emphasizing a weakness of the adult Impalas. An adult Impala is hesitant to use its ability to jump if it is unable to see where it is going to land. This inability to see where it is going to end up at the end of the jump somehow causes an Impala to not act upon something that it is naturally able to do. Let's put it this way, the inability to live by faith, keeps the Impala from doing what God created it to do. With this in mind a three-foot wall put in front of an Impala while its young is able to keep the animal contained because it doesn't see the safety of ground on the other side. So, the African Impala is led to believe while it is still young that it can't do what it was born to do. It grows up to become an adult Impala with the ability to jump into freedom, to live out its purpose, but it won't because it doesn't believe they can. Darrell finished his story right there and said anytime you want to use that in a sermon feel free. I've been connecting that story to every sermon that makes sense to every since.

The Christian life in so many ways is about a series of jumps that can take us higher and further than we are able to go on our own. When I think of jumping higher from a Christian perspective I think about a life of intimacy with and identity in Christ. The Christian life includes, but is not limited to, church attendance and owning a Bible. The Christian life is understanding, the love relationship that God desires to have with us that we become Beloved beings of God. For many to pursue this kind of relationship with God is a jump into the unknown. Grasping a relationship that is meant to be lived by faith can become a 3-foot wall. With God it is possible to jump into the liberating, Spirit-filled life of the Beloved. Some don't take this leap because they are taught something different as a young believer. Maybe they're taught that Christianity is a bunch of rules and if you don't follow the rules, God doesn't love you. Some of these rules may not even be based on Scripture, but because a spiritual leader says so, it must be true. I say this to say, that it's possible to be a Christian and not be free. It's possible to not live in the liberating intimacy that is the Beloved Life.

You can be a Christian and be caged by a 3-foot wall of misinformation fed to you, when you were just a babe in Christ. This could keep one who is Christian from never knowing the freedom of jumping into an intimate relationship with God. One might never take the leap into knowing their spiritu...

JUMP INTO A LIFE OF FURTHER AND HIGHER

EFREM SMITH

Schellhas
Design:
USA

Project: *Typographic/
Photographic*. Art
Director: Hans Schellhas.
Designer: Hans
Schellhas. Client:
Self-authored.

Jose Palma
Visual Works:
Spain

Project: Branding and
brochure design. Art
Director: Jose Palma.
Photo: Laura Jaume.
Designer: Jose Palma.
Client: Perfect
Provisions.

Wonksite Studio:
Colombia

Project: Self promo
posters/workshop.
Art Director: Jorge
Restrepo. Designer:
Jorge Restrepo. Client:
Wonksite Studio.

Unfolding Terrain:
USA

Project: *Died Young
Stayed Pretty* movie
poster. Art Director:
Francheska Guerrero.
Designer: Francheska
Guerrero. Client:
Corcoran College of Art
and Design.

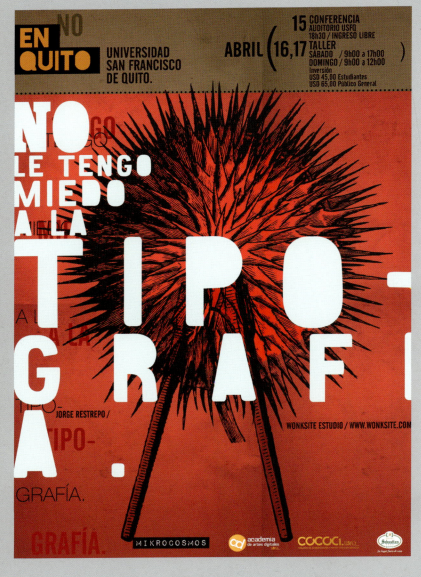

Wonksite Studio:
Colombia

Wonksite Studio:
Colombia

Project: *USA BY DESIGNERS.*
Art Director: Jorge Restrepo.
Designer: Jorge Restrepo.
Client: Hug United.

Project: *1970.* Art
Director: Jorge
Restrepo. Designer:
Jorge Restrepo. Client:
Self-initiated.

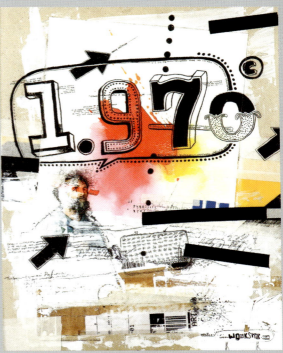

Magma Brand Design:
Germany

Project: *The Denim Bible III*. Art Directors: Lars Harmsen, Jan Kiesswetter, Gian Luca Fracassi. Designers: Christine Bayer, Marc Webers. Client: Sportswear International.

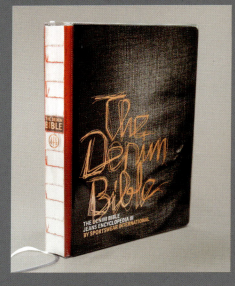

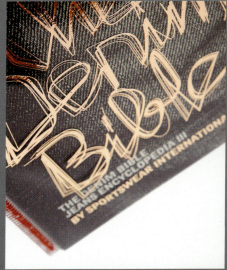

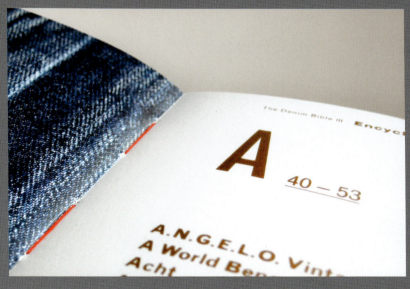

Wonksite Studio:
Colombia

Project: Habla por Haiti
(Talk for Haiti). Art
Director: Jorge
Restrepo. Designers:
Jorge Restrepo, Viviana
Gomez. Client:
Pechakucha Night.

Wonksite Studio:
Colombia

Project: Love. Art
Director: Jorge
Restrepo. Designer:
Jorge Restrepo.
Client: Self-initiated.

Magma Brand Design:
Germany

Project: *Slanted Magazine.*
Art Directors: Lars
Harmsen, Flo Gaertner.
Designer: Julia Kahl.
Client: *Slanted Magazine.*

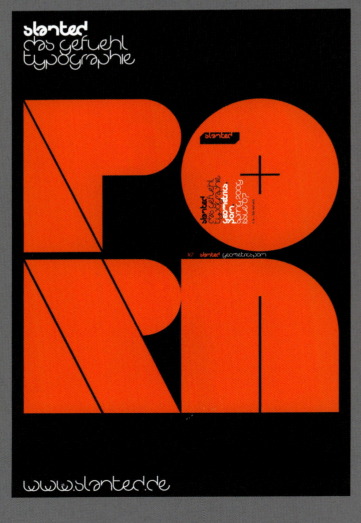

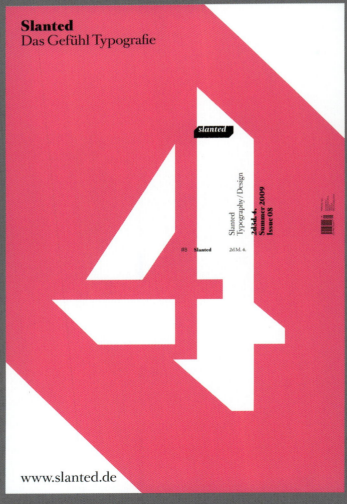

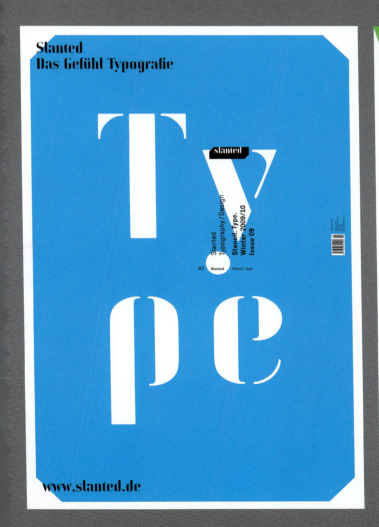

A closer look

Magma Brand Design:
Germany

Slanted Typography / Design

Stencil. Type.
Winter 2009/10
Issue 09

slanted

ISSN 1867-6510
Germany: € 12
Switzerland: CHF 25
UK: £ 16
USA: $ 26
Other Countries: € 16

Slanted Magazine combines the fields of typography, design, illustration, and photography. Each issue of the magazine is dedicated to a special typographic topic, giving each issue a unique quality and making it a collector's piece. The look and layout of each publication reflects the typographic topic in a cutting edge and contemporary way.

A really nice typographic play—once you lay out consecutive issues, the covers tell a different story.

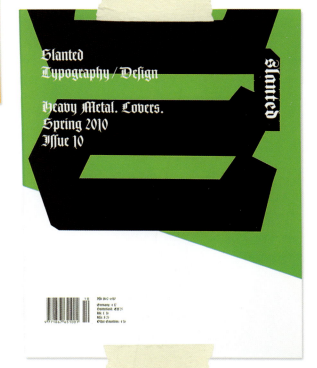

Design nee be reinver time. Now of handwr maybe it's pure Form

Slanted
Heavy Metal. Lovers.
Spring 2010
Issue 10
ISSN 1867-6510

In this context, the typography is almost more important than the content itself, so cropping off sentences is not an issue and provides us with a greater feast for the eyes.

Celebrating more extreme fonts gives Magma the chance to be more edgy and expressive with the typography. In some cases, the type treatments are so wrong, they're right.

Slanted
Typography / Design

Heavy Metal. Lovers.
Spring 2010
Issue 10

slanted

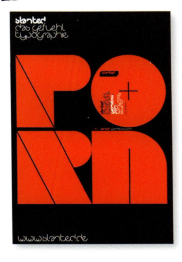

Wonksite Studio:
Colombia

Project: *50 Formas de Ver la Ilustración*. Art Director: Jorge Restrepo. Designer: Jorge Restrepo. Client: {img.} editores.

ISIDRO //// FERRER

Ilustrador, diseñador, cartelista y animador. Cuenta con varias publicaciones en Francia, Portugal y España y una buena cantidad de exposiciones, conferencias y talleres en ciudades como Bruselas, Tokio, México y Bogotá. Así como importantes premios.

ME ACUERDO }

Para todo amor hay un primer instante.

Me acuerdo de mi primera caja de lápices de colores de la marca "alpino", era una caja básica de 12 colores que para mí constituía un tesoro. Los primeros días me contentaba con mirar los colores alineados y ordenados, me resistía a usarlos por temor a desgastar sus puntas encendidas. Me acuerdo de las cajas de lápices que sucedieron a la primera y cómo los colores se fueron consumiendo a oleadas como un mar agitado que erosiona las orillas. Me acuerdo de mi tía Soledad afilando los lápices con una tajadera metálica, un instrumento que hace tiempo desapareció de las papelerías y que era la versión infantil de la guillotina. Me acuerdo del sonido de la cuchilla de acero al rasgar la madera, un sonido que me helaba los dientes y me erizaba la piel con una mezcla de sensaciones contradictorias. Me acuerdo de la angustia que me producía sacar punta a los lápices e ir perdiendo por el exceso de celo uno tras otro fragmentos de mina que obstruían el sacapuntas y consumían el lapicero hasta convertirlo en proyectil inservible. Me acuerdo del olor a madera de lápiz, un olor que me ha acompañado toda la vida, un olor que para don Ramón Gómez de la Serna es el único que puede competir con el olor a tormenta. Me acuerdo de que a los lápices de colores le siguieron los rotuladores, y a estos las ceras, y a estas las temperas, y las acuarelas, y la tinta china y las cartulinas pantone... Yo sigo aferrado al lápiz y cuando escribo estas líneas lo hago sombreando de grafito las palabras. El lápiz está tan pegado a los dedos que con el uso viene a ser uno más de ellos, viene a formar parte del todo que es

« ABC / ISIDRO FERRER

Cuando estoy pintando, tengo la costumbre de hacer café para dos, incluso
cuando estoy sola. Creo que me hace sentir acompañado.

.01

FELIPE)
BEDOYA

ILUSTRADOR
ESTUDIANTE DE DISEÑO GRÁFICO / BELLAS ARTES DE CALI
CALI / COLOMBIA
WWW.FELIPEBEDOYA.COM

– pg. 32 .30
/// kal.quadra@ymail.com

LAURA OSORNO
www.lauraosorno.net

– pg. 46 .44
/// lauraosorno@gmail.com

(2001).

Ilustr
Bogotá.
Uni

DISEÑO /
+ WEBSITE STUDIO

DIRECCIÓN DE ARTE /
JORGE RESTREPO

DIAGRAMACIÓN Y ARMADA /
DIEGO VELÁSQUEZ
EDUARDO PALMA
VIVIANA GÓMEZ

CORRECCIÓN DE ESTILO /
DIANA ARIAS
CLAUDIA LUQUE

IMPRESO EN COLOMBIA POR /
TORREBLANCA AG

PATROCINADO POR /
CIFRAS & CONCEPTOS S.A.

COLABORADORES /
MIGUEL BUSTOS
DIANA MURCIA
YUBERLEY APONTE
PAULA BERNAL

AGRADECIMIENTOS /
CÉSAR CABALLERO / DIANA CASTELLANOS /
ISIDRO FERRER / OSCAR COLA
CARMEN ELISA DIAZ / MARÍA REINA
ILUSTRADORES COLOMBIANOS.COM
TINTOGTINTA

APOYAN /
Cámara
Colombiana
del Libro
& CIFRAS & CONCEPTOS
Información Inteligente

ISBN: 978-958-44-7126-0

dos. Prohibida la reproducción total o parcial en cualquier
los titulares del copyright y de los autores de cada una
nes aquí presentadas. Publicación sin valor comercial.

///

Dibujante desde hace años, comenzó sus estudios en Historia
en la Universidad Nacional de Colombia en el 2004 y en el 2008
decidió cambiar de rumbo. Desde entonces es estudiante de Diseño de Vestuario y Escenografía en la Universidad de Artes de
Berlín- Weißensee.
Ha participado en exposiciones en el Museo de Arte Contem-
poráneo de Bogotá (2004), en la Galería Colombiana de Diseño
(2007), y en el Archivo de Bogotá (2007).
Hizo ilustraciones para los libros Árquiem y Der Rote Stier de
Tilman Geishaser, participó en proyectos como Re952+Project
2008 y Postales Pour Designer Edition 2009, entre otros.

A

ALEX SARMIENTO – pg. 26 .26
www.flickr.com/theaparels/ /// theaparels@gmail.com

ANITA TORRES – pg. 17 .15
www.anitatorres.com /// anitatorres@yahoo.com

Diseñador Gráfico de la Universidad Nacional de Colombia. Se
ha dedicado a la ilustración y el diseño desde el 2005, desem-
peñándose en el campo publicitario, institucional y con ONGs.
Como ilustrador ha trabajado, para diferentes publicaciones
exposiciones tanto análogas como digitales. En el 2008 participó
en la exposición Colombia Passion en Hong Kong y en el 2009 en
Drawing Dreams en Berkeley.
Actualmente incursiona en el campo de la narrativa gráfica.

Artista Visual y Diseñadora Gráfica de la Universidad Jorge
Tadeo Lozano. Empezó a ilustrar libros para niños, jóvenes y
adultos hace siete años. Ha trabajado para editoriales como:
Hispanoamérica, Educar, Panamericana Editorial, Casa Editorial
El Tiempo, Revista Bacanika, entre otras.
En los últimos cuatro años su trabajo se ha centrado en el diseño, la ilustración editorial, el street art y las artes plásticas.
Ha participado en más de diez exposiciones en su país y en el
exterior. En el 2007 obtuvo el premio Encourage en La Bienal
Internacional de Roma, Japón, por un proyecto editorial ilustra-
do. Ha sido docente universitaria durante cinco años.
Con su trabajo de murales ha participado en propuestas so-
ciales lideradas por la Alcaldía de Bogotá como Graffiti Mujer,
en el festival: Cámara, Luces, Mujeres en Acción,
en Colombia y Argentina. Actualmente vive en Buenos Aires y
continúa con su trabajo de ilustración. Además realiza una serie
de murales bajo el seudónimo 1000+e. Cursa estudios de Historia
del Arte del Siglo XIX y Medios Digitales.

AMALIA SATIZÁBAL – pg. 31 .31
www.amaliasatizabal.com /// amaliasatizabal@gmail.com

ANDRÉS CANO – pg. 05 .03
/// andrescano@gmail.com

Burge Agency:
UK

Project: Bomber,
Torpedo, Grenade,
and Bullet shot glass
branding. Designer: Paul
Burgess. Client: Entice.

Alex Trochut:
Spain

**Project: "10 Ways to
Get a Job". Art
Director: Alex Trochut.
Client: *Computer Arts*
magazine.**

Project: Latino America.
Art Director: Jorge
Restrepo. Designer:
Jorge Restrepo. Client:
Antifichus book (Pequeño
Editor Press).

WORKtoDATE:
USA

Project: *Recharge*,
an event poster designed
to promote The Art
Institute of York PA
Annual Alumni Exhibit.
Art Director: Greg
Bennett. Designer: Greg
Bennett. Client: The Art
Institute of York
Pennsylvania.

Wonksite Studio:
Colombia

Project: *Colombiage 11*.
Art Director: Jorge
Restrepo. Designer:
Jorge Restrepo. Client:
Colombiage.

Uretsky & Co:
USA

Project: Download cover
art for net-release EP.
Art Director: Jan Audun
Uretsky. Designer: Jan
Audun Uretsky. Client:
Julien Mier.

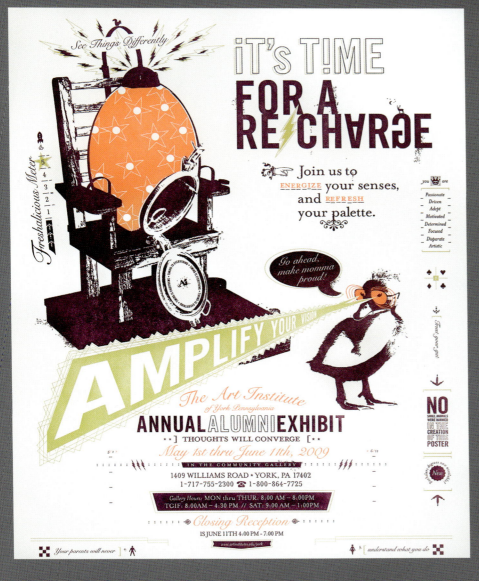

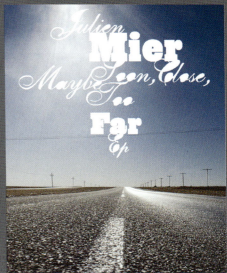

Magma Brand Design:
Germany

Project: *Typodarium
2012 The Daily Dose of
Typography*. Art Director:
Boris Kahl. Designers:
Lars Harmsen, Raban
Ruddigkeit. Client:
Hermann Schmidt
Mainz.

Magma Brand Design:
Germany

Project: *TypoShirt One.*
Art Directors: Lars
Harmsen, Philipp
Louven. Designers:
Lars Harmsen, Philipp
Louven. Client: Index
Book, S.L.

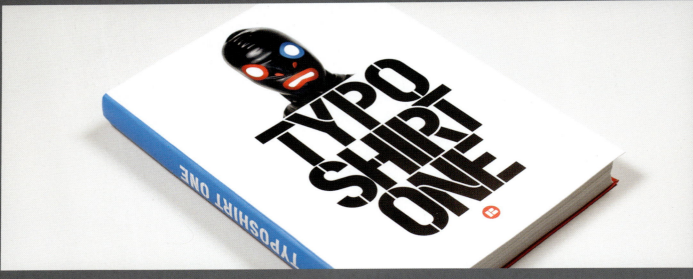

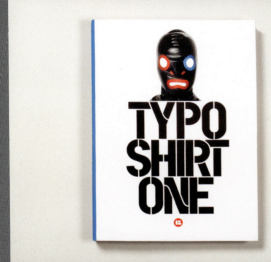

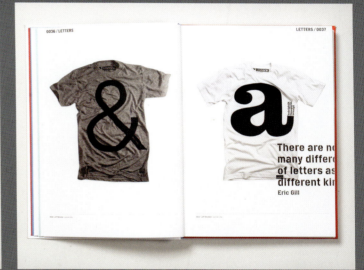

Sensus Design
Factory Zagreb:
Croatia

Project: Robert Pauletta
Poster. Art Director:
Nedjeljko Spoljar.
Designers: Nedjeljko
Spoljar, Kristina Spoljar.
Client: Galerija Klovicevi
dvori.

Robert
Pauletta

**Astra
Anonima**

Galerija
Klovicevi
dvori

Jezultski trg 4
Zagreb

17 12 02 ___ 19 01 03

Wonksite Studio:
Colombia

Project: Clock. Art
Director: Jorge
Restrepo. Designer:
Jorge Restrepo. Client:
mySHELF project.

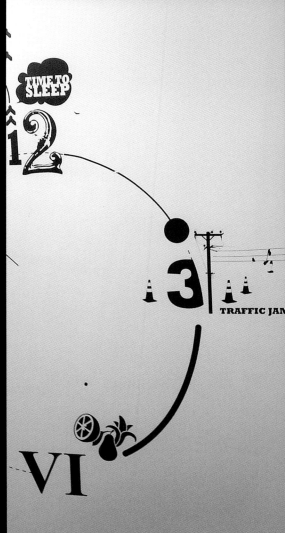

Project: Ministry of Fish
branding and postcards.
Designer: Paul Burgess.
Client: Ministry of Fish.

Silver Lining
Design:
USA

Project: Self-promotion
for designer. Art
Director: Trisha Leavitt.
Designer: Trisha Leavitt.
Client: Trisha Leavitt.

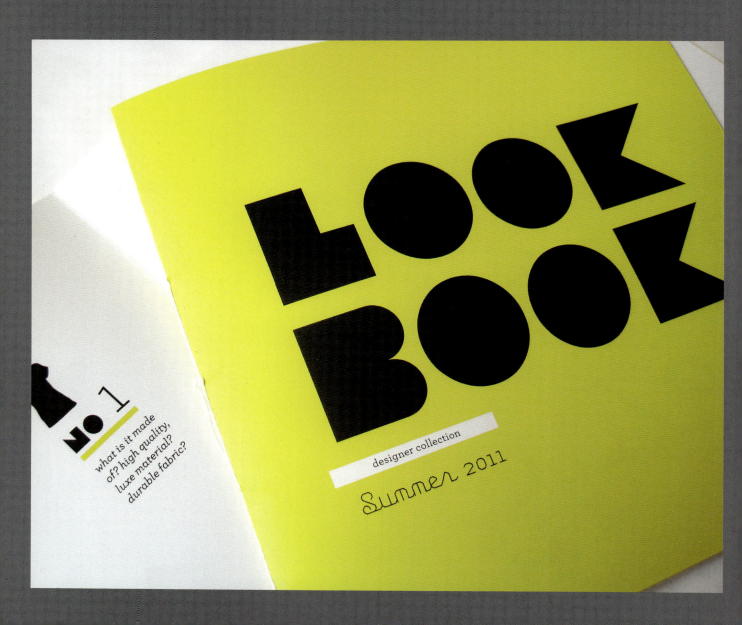

Unfolding Terrain: USA

Project: Seymour Chwast lecture poster. Art Director: Francheska Guerrero. Designer: Francheska Guerrero. Client: Corcoran College of Art and Design.

Unfolding Terrain: USA

Project: Marian Bantjes Lecture Poster. Art Director: Francheska Guerrero. Designer: Francheska Guerrero. Client: Corcoran College of Art and Design.

Un Mundo Feliz: Spain

Project: Digital image against fashion's fascism. Art Directors: Sonia Díaz, Gabriel Martínez. Designer: Gabriel Martínez. Client: UMF.

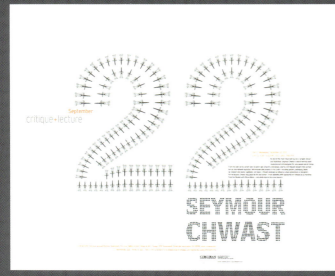

I Love Dust:
UK

I Love Dust:
UK

Project: Peep Peep Don't
Sleep (our favourite
studio slogans in 3D).
Art Directors: Ben
Beach, Mark Graham.
Designer: I Love Dust.
Client: I Love Dust.

Project: Doves: Lyric
posters. Art Directors: Ben
Beach, Mark Graham.
Designer: I Love Dust.
Client: I Love Dust.

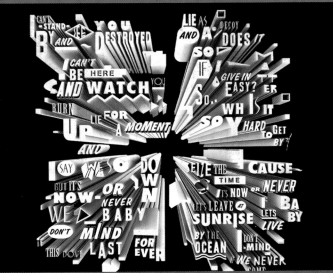

The Allotment:
Mongolia

Project: Brand creation
and self-promotion
materials for The
Allotment. Art Directors:
James Backhurst,
Michael Smith, Paula
Talford, Paul Middlebrook.
Designers: James
Backhurst, Michael
Smith, Paula Talford,
Paul Middlebrook. Client:
The Allotment.

Sensus Design Factory Zagreb: Croatia

Project: *Snapshot* posters. Art Director: Nedjeljko Spoljar. Designers: Nedjeljko Spoljar, Kristina Spoljar. Client: Galerija Klovicevi dvori.

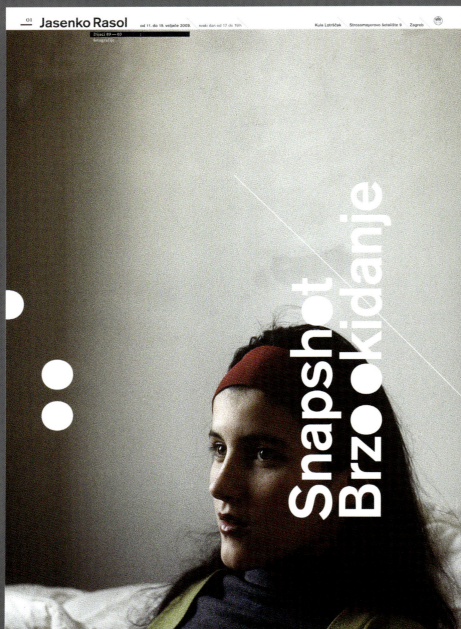

Brigada:
Croatia

Project: Zavrtnica
Typotecture. Architect:
Damjan Geber. Product
Designer: Srdana Alač.
Designer: Branimir
Sabljić. Client: B.M.V.
inzenjering.

A closer look

Brigada:
Croatia

The architects and designers of Croatia's Brigada agency designed a striking and economical solution to restore Zagreb's Zavrtnica business center. What's interesting is that an entire block with four structures was treated as a whole. The design team used "typotecture" to minimize refurbishing costs and create a fresh, new look to the existing structures.

It's certainly a brave and very bold move to cover large buildings in type. It may not be to everyone's taste, but it is a really interesting concept. And leaves one asking, "Why not?"

Throwing type into total disarray, with characters balancing awkwardly on top of one another is an interesting approach to typography, but making the strange imbalance work on structures of this size makes the typography that much more impressive.

Un Mundo Feliz:
Spain

Project: NO poster.
Art Directors: Sonia Díaz, Gabriel Martínez. Designer: Gabriel Martínez. Client: MUSAC Contemporary Art Center.

Un Mundo Feliz:
Spain

Project: Postcard series. Art Directors: Sonia Díaz, Gabriel Martínez. Designer: Gabriel Martínez. Client: UIMP.

Alex Trochut:
Spain

Project: Go for it. Art Director: Alex Trochut. Client: If you could.

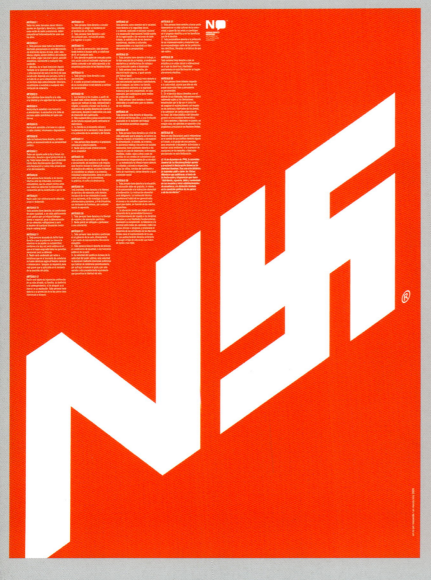

Un Mundo
Feliz:
Spain

Project: Poster. Art
Directors: Sonia Díaz,
Gabriel Martínez.
Designer: Gabriel
Martínez. The poster
project for Palestine.

Marshall Rake:
USA

Project: Promotional
accordian-fold brochure/
poster for Katalyst. Art
Director: Rachel Ma.
Designer: Marshall Rake.
Client: Katalyst.

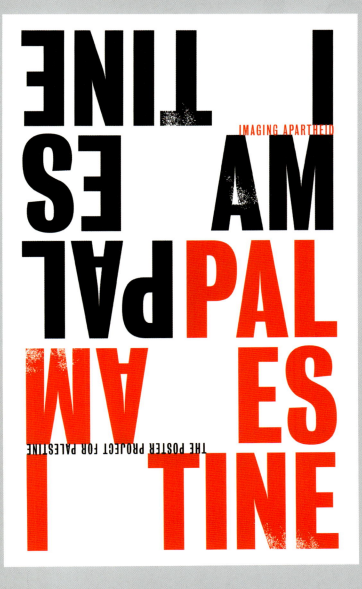

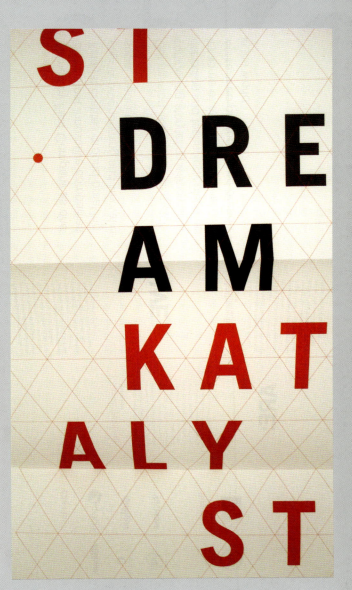

Free-form: Type

Chapter 5

Embracing imperfection.

In light of the freeform nature of hand lettering, I'll try to keep my thoughts organic and free as that would only be fair, given the subject matter. Why do I like hand-drawn typography? What inspires me? Why do I think hand lettering is important when used in the right situations? I guess I've never really thought about the answers to these questions. Art school always seemed to focus on establishing excellence in traditional computer-based typography. Maybe the reason that I enjoy hand-drawn lettering so much is because it is uncharted territory, where the rules pertaining to traditional typography can be broken. As different as hand lettering appears to be at times, a foundation in typography is an absolute necessity—but you already knew that.

I have always been an avid fan of hand lettering primarily because it adds a human side to an otherwise computer-dominated era of typography. Computer fonts can sometimes have limitations, whereas the free-form "break all the rules" aesthetic of hand-drawn typography can provide a useful solution for the right project. For instance, it's not too often that you can switch typefaces in the middle of a thought without it looking completely out of place; whereas, hand lettering is defined by "malpractices" such as these. Don't get me wrong, I love computers and their seemingly infinite well of fonts that obviously play a huge role in any designer's workflow, but it is important to understand when to use them and for what kinds of projects.

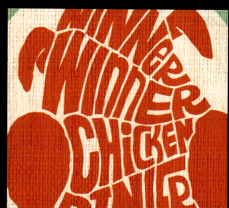

Before computers, the craft of hand lettering was much more widespread. The arrival of postscript fonts and desktop computing caused it drop out of favor to a degree and hand lettering was the last thing anyone was interested in, but it is currently experiencing a popular revival. This new hand-lettering revolution could be a result of the dust settling on the excitement that grew up around the technological era and all things digital. If anything, hand lettering has the ability to reveal the hand of its creator and at a minimum, convey a sense of gestural human craft. Although working by hand can be extremely time inefficient, the finished product always has a unique quality that stands on its own.

I love describing my style as embraced imperfection. Being a perfectionist, it was not until I learned how to accept the crooked lines, misaligned type, and illegibility that my lettering took on character and interest. As odd as it seems, these imperfections can have just as much craft as perfection. If you look at any great hand-lettering artist's work, you will see these "errors" are not accidents at all.

I have always felt that my lettering projects and daily drawings reflect the world and its many inspirations from my own perspective. There isn't a day that goes by where I don't see or hear something that inspires me, which is why I keep a list of neverending thoughts and phrases that I plan to draw— all inspired by my every day life. I like to think that viewing an artist's hand lettering can tell you a lot about him or her when taking into consideration the style and content. Since music and art are a huge part of who I am, my lettering is primarily a fusion of those two subjects, which in turn allows me to keep a certain dedication and passion behind my work. Then again, the connection between music and hand lettering is nothing new—just look at the infinite amount of band posters, flyers, and shirts out there. It's overwhelming and ridiculously inspiring!

Aside from my own inspirations, something needs to be said about the importance of looking at and studying all of the other art out there, especially those styles relevant to your own. In retrospect, I can't tell you how many artists (many of whom are featured in this book) have played an integral role in the evolution of my own work. Their passion and dedication is palpable, and that is contagious.

Project: T-Shirt & Sneaks.
Art Director: Jay Roeder.
Designer: Jay Roeder.

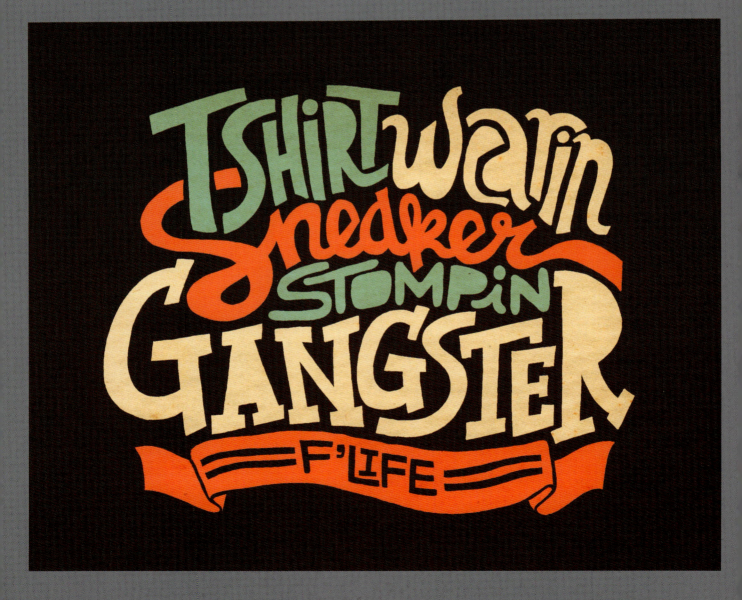

Jay Roeder:
USA

Project: Lower Case G.
Art Director: Jay Roeder.
Designer: Jay Roeder.

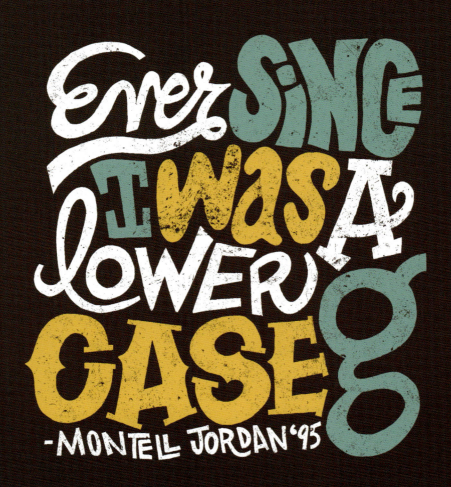

**Jay
Roeder:**
USA

**Alex
Trochut:**
Spain

Project: Inspired Since '84.
Art Director: Jay Roeder.
Designer: Jay Roeder.

Project: Proposal for the
Cadbury's print campaign.
Art Director: Alex Trochut.

Jay Roeder: USA

Jay Roeder: USA

Extra Black: Graphic Design Studio: USA

Project: Brooklyn Scribble. Art Director: Jay Roeder. Designer: Jay Roeder.

Project: Winner Winner. Art Director: Jay Roeder. Designer: Jay Roeder.

Project: T-shirt design contest call for entries for Ed Kemp Associates 50th anniverary event: JamFest. Art Director: David McLawhorn. Designer: David McLawhorn. Client: Ed Kemp Associates.

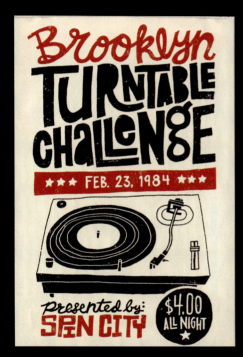

Project: *344 Questions:
The creative person's
do-it-yourself guide to
insight, survival, and
artistic fulfillment.* Art
Director: Stefan G.
Bucher. Client: Peachpit/
New Riders.

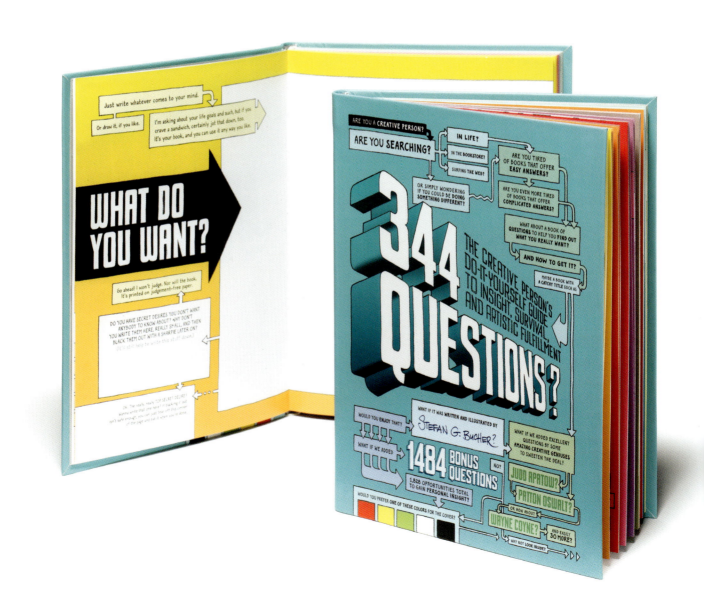

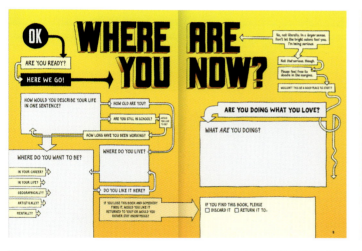

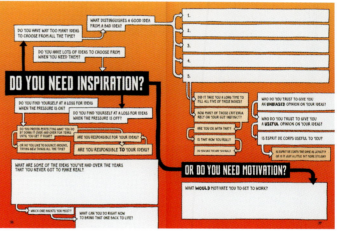

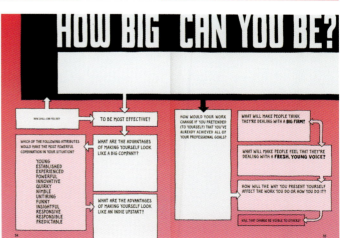

A closer look

344 Design:
USA

A veritable therapy session on paper, *344 Questions* is designed to help you determine where you are in your life and career, where you want to be, and how to get there. Hopefully, you'll also laugh along the way. Each spread in this colorful, pocket-sized book contains a series of several questions illustrated in Stefan Bucher's unique, whimsical, hand-lettered style. The questions are designed to get you thinking, drawing, and writing, with room on each spread to fill in the blanks and jot down ideas. In addition to the questions provided by Bucher, the book features questions from creative celebrities who share some of the questions they were asked on the way to success or in some cases, the questions they wish they had been asked.

What happens when you combine precision with imprecision? It would probably look a little like this!

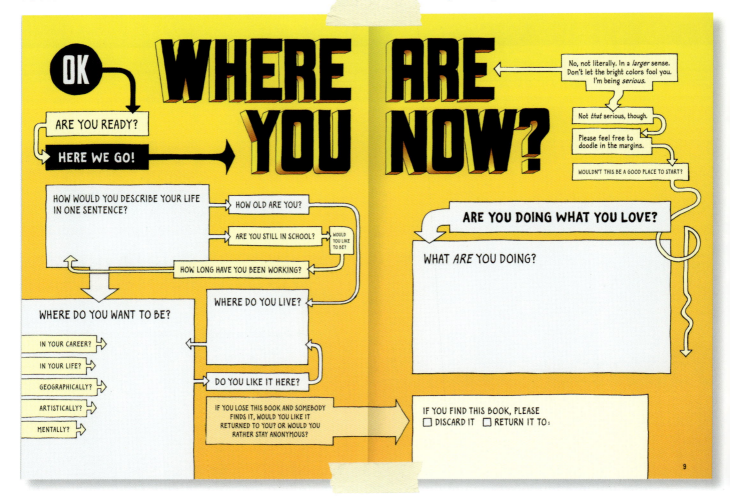

OK

ARE YOU READY?

HERE WE GO!

WHERE YOU ARE NOW?

No, not literally. In a *larger* sense. Don't let the bright colors fool you. I'm being *serious*.

Not *that* serious, though.

Please feel free to doodle in the margins.

WOULDN'T THIS BE A GOOD PLACE TO START?

HOW WOULD YOU DESCRIBE YOUR LIFE IN ONE SENTENCE?

HOW OLD ARE YOU?

ARE YOU STILL IN SCHOOL?

WOULD YOU LIKE TO BE?

HOW LONG HAVE YOU BEEN WORKING?

WHERE DO YOU LIVE?

ARE YOU DOING WHAT YOU LOVE?

WHAT *ARE* YOU DOING?

WHERE DO YOU WANT TO BE?

IN YOUR CAREER?

IN YOUR LIFE?

GEOGRAPHICALLY?

ARTISTICALLY?

MENTALLY?

DO YOU LIKE IT HERE?

IF YOU LOSE THIS BOOK AND SOMEBODY FINDS IT, WOULD YOU LIKE IT RETURNED TO YOU? OR WOULD YOU RATHER STAY ANONYMOUS?

IF YOU FIND THIS BOOK, PLEASE ☐ DISCARD IT ☐ RETURN IT TO:

9

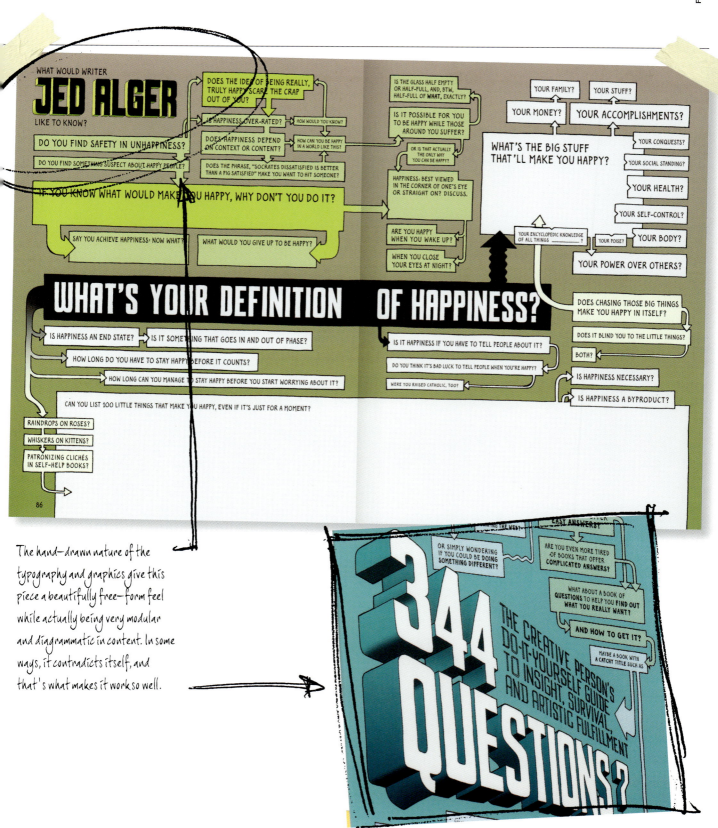

WHAT WOULD WRITER
JED ALGER
LIKE TO KNOW?

DO YOU FIND SAFETY IN UNHAPPINESS?

DO YOU FIND SOMETHING SUSPECT ABOUT HAPPY PEOPLE?

IF YOU KNOW WHAT WOULD MAKE YOU HAPPY, WHY DON'T YOU DO IT?

SAY YOU ACHIEVE HAPPINESS: NOW WHAT?

WHAT WOULD YOU GIVE UP TO BE HAPPY?

DOES THE IDEA OF BEING REALLY, TRULY HAPPY SCARE THE CRAP OUT OF YOU?

IS HAPPINESS OVER-RATED?

HOW WOULD YOU KNOW?

DOES HAPPINESS DEPEND ON CONTEXT OR CONTENT?

HOW CAN YOU BE HAPPY IN A WORLD LIKE THIS?

DOES THE PHRASE, "SOCRATES DISSATISFIED IS BETTER THAN A PIG SATISFIED" MAKE YOU WANT TO HIT SOMEONE?

IS THE GLASS HALF EMPTY OR HALF-FULL, AND, BTW, HALF-FULL OF WHAT, EXACTLY?

IS IT POSSIBLE FOR YOU TO BE HAPPY WHILE THOSE AROUND YOU SUFFER?

OR IS THAT ACTUALLY THE ONLY WAY YOU CAN BE HAPPY?

HAPPINESS: BEST VIEWED IN THE CORNER OF ONE'S EYE OR STRAIGHT ON? DISCUSS.

ARE YOU HAPPY WHEN YOU WAKE UP?

WHEN YOU CLOSE YOUR EYES AT NIGHT?

YOUR FAMILY?

YOUR STUFF?

YOUR MONEY?

YOUR ACCOMPLISHMENTS?

WHAT'S THE BIG STUFF THAT'LL MAKE YOU HAPPY?

YOUR CONQUESTS?

YOUR SOCIAL STANDING?

YOUR HEALTH?

YOUR SELF-CONTROL?

YOUR ENCYCLOPEDIC KNOWLEDGE OF ALL THINGS _____ ?

YOUR POISE?

YOUR BODY?

YOUR POWER OVER OTHERS?

WHAT'S YOUR DEFINITION OF HAPPINESS?

IS HAPPINESS AN END STATE?

IS IT SOMETHING THAT GOES IN AND OUT OF PHASE?

HOW LONG DO YOU HAVE TO STAY HAPPY BEFORE IT COUNTS?

HOW LONG CAN YOU MANAGE TO STAY HAPPY BEFORE YOU START WORRYING ABOUT IT?

CAN YOU LIST 100 LITTLE THINGS THAT MAKE YOU HAPPY, EVEN IF IT'S JUST FOR A MOMENT?

RAINDROPS ON ROSES?

WHISKERS ON KITTENS?

PATRONIZING CLICHÉS IN SELF-HELP BOOKS?

IS IT HAPPINESS IF YOU HAVE TO TELL PEOPLE ABOUT IT?

DO YOU THINK IT'S BAD LUCK TO TELL PEOPLE WHEN YOU'RE HAPPY?

WERE YOU RAISED CATHOLIC, TOO?

DOES CHASING THOSE BIG THINGS MAKE YOU HAPPY IN ITSELF?

DOES IT BLIND YOU TO THE LITTLE THINGS?

BOTH?

IS HAPPINESS NECESSARY?

IS HAPPINESS A BYPRODUCT?

86

The hand-drawn nature of the typography and graphics give this piece a beautifully free-form feel while actually being very modular and diagrammatic in content. In some ways, it contradicts itself, and that's what makes it work so well.

... THE WEST?

OR SIMPLY WONDERING IF YOU COULD BE DOING SOMETHING DIFFERENT?

EASY ANSWERS?

ARE YOU EVEN MORE TIRED OF BOOKS THAT OFFER COMPLICATED ANSWERS?

WHAT ABOUT A BOOK OF QUESTIONS TO HELP YOU FIND OUT WHAT YOU REALLY WANT?

AND HOW TO GET IT?

MAYBE A BOOK WITH A CATCHY TITLE SUCH AS

344 QUESTIONS?

THE CREATIVE PERSON'S DO-IT-YOURSELF GUIDE TO INSIGHT, SURVIVAL, AND ARTISTIC FULFILLMENT

VISUALMENTALSTIMULI:
USA

Project: *Wordscapes of Western Pennsylvania*, a series of silk-screen prints that visualizes Western PA's unique way of speaking, and explores the 'typographic landscape' of the region. Art Director: David Kasparek. Designer: David Kasparek. Client: Self-initiated.

344 Design:
USA

Project: Spelling Bee
poster. Art Director:
Stefan G. Bucher.
Client: 826la.org.

Another Limited
Rebellion:
USA

Project: Lisa Moore CD
package. Art Director:
Noah Scalin. Designer:
Noah Scalin. Client:
Cantaloupe Music.

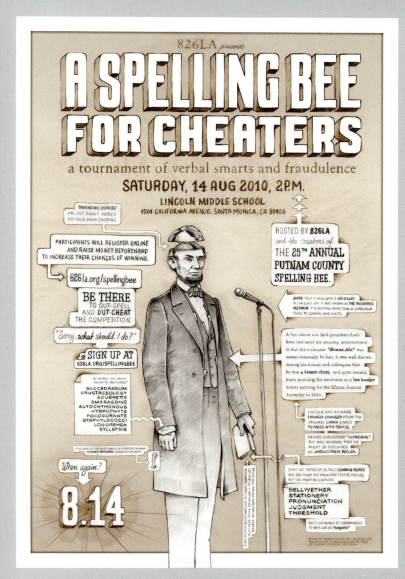

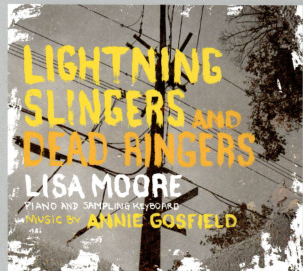

Sophia Georgopoulou: Greece

Project: Plant your dreams and let them grow (self-promotion packaging). Art Director: Sophia Georgopoulou. Client: Sophia Georgopoulou.

Project: Blink-182.
Art Director: Jay Roeder.
Designer: Jay Roeder.

Elliott Burford:
USA

Project: Le Sac.
Designer: Elliott Burford.
Client: Benetton.

Elliott Burford:
USA

Project: Window display.
Art Director: Sam Baron.
Designer: Elliott Burford.
Client: Monoprix.

A closer look

Jay Roeder:
USA

What's so exciting about this work is that it's never been anywhere near a computer. It's totally free-form, totally the work of one man's hand and a couple of pens.

Often free-form work is distinguishable by the person who did it. It has that person's hallmark all over it, his style of typography. But this piece relishes in being totally diverse, every piece of type being in some way different, as if drawn my many different hands.

It may look like fairly random doodling, but to create typography quite so imperfect, you have to know your stuff. To intentionally get perspectives wrong, characters incorrect, and generally allow the mind to do things it's trained not to takes immense skill—and a slightly warped brain, I suspect!

Project: "ink & circumstance". Art Director: Stefan G. Bucher. Designers: Emily Potts, Tom Biederback. Client: *STEP Inside Design* magazine.

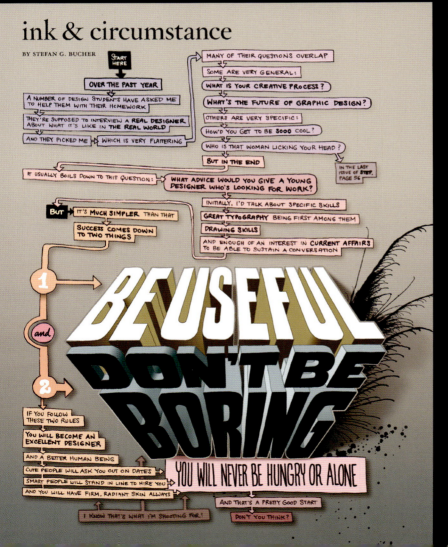

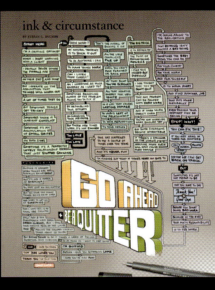

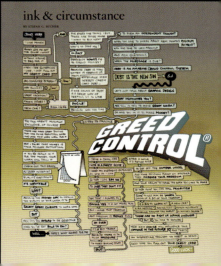

Shawn Sanem:
USA

Project: Bud Prize Poster 2010. Designer: Shawn Sanem. Client: Helix.

Go Welsh:
USA

Project: Call for entries poster series: Volume 4. Art Director: Craig Welsh. Designer: Scott Marz. Client: Music For Everyone.

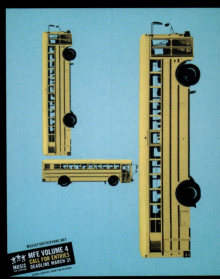

Sophy Lee Design:
USA

Project: *Cinderela*, a
book cover for the adult
version of *Cinderela*,
made from old clothes.
Art Director: Sophy Lee.
Designer: Sophy Lee.
Client: MFA, School of
Visual Arts.

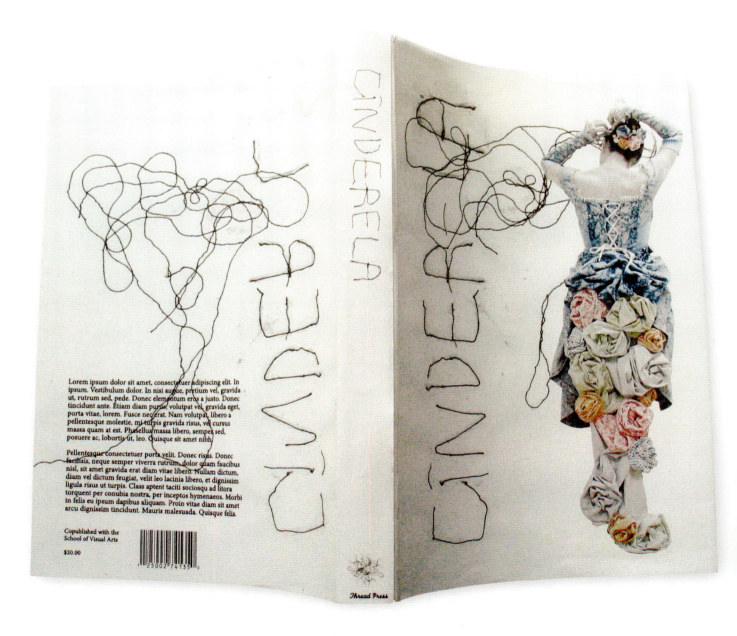

Lorem ipsum dolor sit amet, consectetuer adipiscing elit. In ipsum. Vestibulum dolor. In nisi augue, pretium vel, gravida ut, rutrum sed, pede. Donec elementum eros a justo. Donec tincidunt ante. Etiam diam purus, volutpat vel, gravida eget, porta vitae, lorem. Fusce necerat. Nam volutpat, libero a pellentesque molestie, mi turpis gravida risus, vel cursus massa quam at est. Phasellus massa libero, semper sed, posuere ac, lobortis ut, leo. Quisque sit amet nibh.

Pellentesque consectetuer porta velit. Donec risus. Donec facilisis, neque semper viverra rutrum dolor quam faucibus nisl, sit amet gravida erat diam vitae libero. Nullam dictum, diam vel dictum feugiat, velit leo lacinia libero, et dignissim ligula risus ut turpis. Class aptent taciti sociosqu ad litora torquent per conubia nostra, per inceptos hymenaeos. Morbi in felis eu ipsum dapibus aliquam. Proin vitae diam sit amet arcu dignissim tincidunt. Mauris malesuada. Quisque felis.

Copublished with the
School of Visual Arts

$20.00

CINDERELA

Thread Press

Bowling Green State University
School of Art Graphic Design Division:
USA

Project: Input/Output
2011 AIGA Toledo/
BGSUGD Portfolio
Review Day poster.
Art Director: Associate
Professor Matt Davis.
Designer: Morgan
Swedburg. Client: AIGA
Toledo/BGSUGD.

input: it's THE STUFF you think, the ideas YOU DREAM, THE things YOU'RE taught, the late nights & WILD brainstorming, THE YOUTHFUL Exploration, AND THE determination & passion to Create SOMETHING completely NEW

Scorsone/
Drueding:
USA

Project: Poster for Haiti Poster Project to raise money for the earthquake victims. Art Directors: Joe Scorsone, Alice Drueding. Designers: Joe Scorsone, Alice Drueding. Client: The Haiti Poster Project.

Scorsone/
Drueding:
USA

Project: CO_2 emissions awareness poster. Art Directors: Joe Scorsone, Alice Drueding. Designers: Joe Scorsone, Alice Drueding. Client: Good 50x70 Poster Competition.

HELP HAITI

HAITIAN EARTHQUAKE VICTIMS DESPERATELY NEED PROSTHETIC DEVICES.

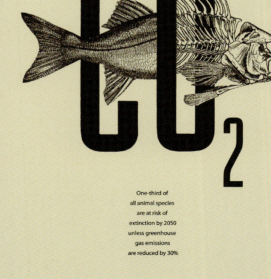

One-third of all animal species are at risk of extinction by 2050 unless greenhouse gas emissions are reduced by 30%

Un Mundo Feliz:
Spain

Project: Poster. Art
Directors: Sonia Díaz,
Gabriel Martínez.
Designer: Gabriel
Martínez. Client: The
Haiti Poster Project.

Kiku Obata
& Company:
USA

Project: Dr. Scholl's
Shoes Spring 2012 look
look. Art Director: Kiku
Obata. Designers: Amy
Knopf, Kristen Malone,
Paul Scherfling, Carlos
Zamora. Client: Dr.
Scholl's Shoes.

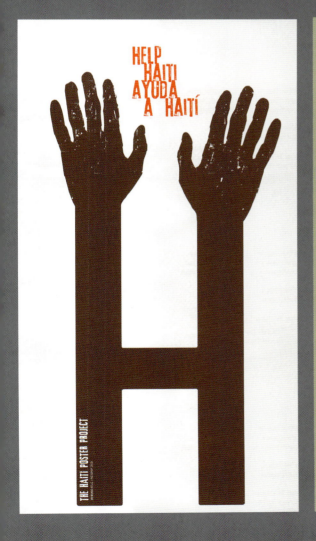

DR. SCHOLL'S® SHOES
SPRING SUMMER 2012
american getaway
ENDLESS DAYS UNDER THE SUN
EVERYWHERE IN BLOOM
WORK & PLAY
FOREVER AT EASE
MEN'S AND WOMEN'S ✳ CASUALS AND ATHLETICS

344 Design:
USA

Project: *100 Days of Monsters.* Art Director: Stefan G. Bucher. Client: Peachpit/New Riders.

Project: CD package for Stew's soundtrack for *A Midsummer Night's Dream*. Art Director: Noah Scalin. Designer: Noah Scalin. Client: Shakespeare on The Sound.

Project: Passion Coalition logo. Art Director: Noah Scalin. Designer: Noah Scalin. Client: Epic Theatre Ensemble.

Project: JDUB logo. Art Director: Noah Scalin. Designer: Noah Scalin. Client: JDUB.

Project: The Play Company logo. Art Director: Noah Scalin. Designer: Noah Scalin. Client: The Play Company.

a midsumm night's dream

stew

Joe Miller's
Company:
USA

Project: *Caesura*
journal series.
Designer: Joe Miller.
Client: Poetry Center
San Jose.

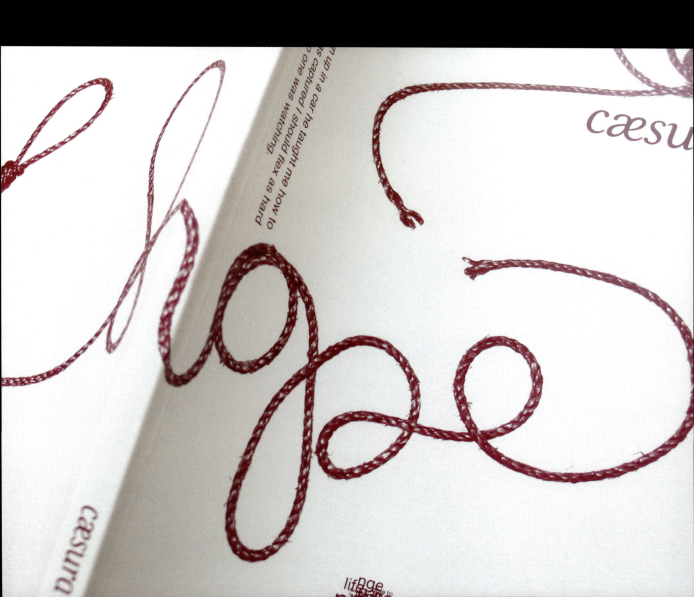

Project: Synthesis
Center corporate
identity. Art Director:
Sophia Georgopoulou.
Designer: Sophia
Georgopoulou. Client:
Aneta Alexandridi.

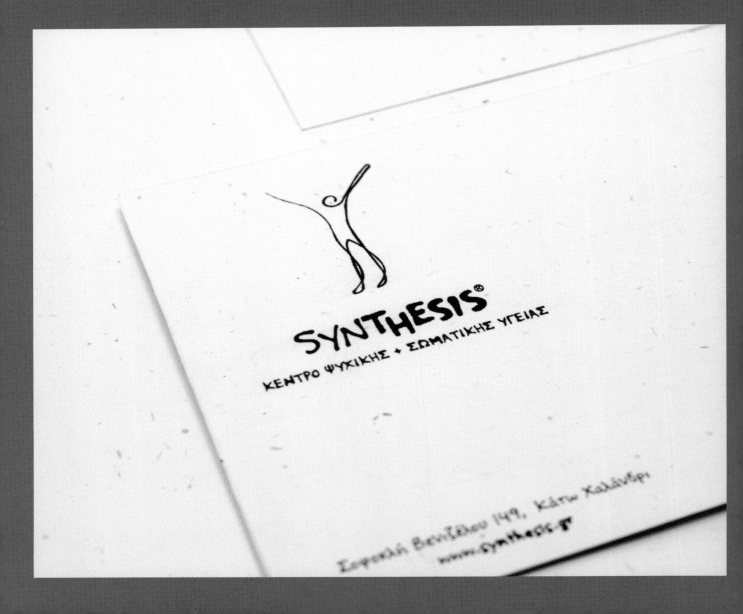

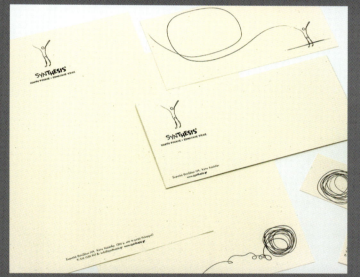

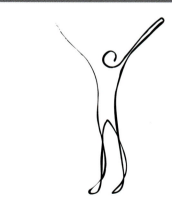

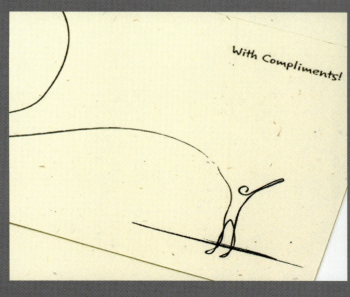

Project: High Priority
Monsters, illustration.
Art Director: Rob Hewitt.
Designer: Stefan G.
Bucher. Client: *New York
Magazine*.

344 Design:
USA

344 Design:
USA

Project: *I Found This
Funny* Poster. Art
Director: Stefan G.
Bucher. Client: 826la.org.

Project: *L A Weekly*
cover. Art Director:
Stefan G. Bucher. Client:
L A Weekly.

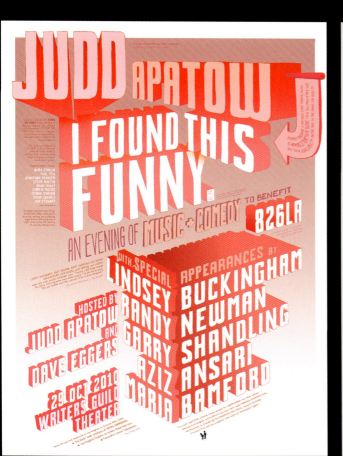

Bruketa & Žinić:
Croatia

Project: *Spam Jam*.
Creative Directors:
Davor Bruketa, Nikola
Žinić. Art Director,
Designer, Illustrator:
Nebojša Cvetković.
Copywriter: Tonči Klarić.
Client: Igrepa grupa.

**Steers McGillan
Eves Design:**
UK

Project: Publicity
material for Bath
International Literature
Festival. Art Director:
Richard McGillan.
Designer: Dan Weeks.
Client: Bath Festivals.

LitFest

Steer/McColl an Design Ltd 0225 465546

Bath festivals

Bath Festivals
Box Office
2 Church Street,
Abbey Green,
Bath BA1 1NL

Tickets
01225 463362
www.bathlitfest.org.uk

Tickets: 01225 463362
www.bathlitfest.org.uk

Bath festivals

Sat 27
February –
Sun 7
March

BATH
LITERATURE
FESTIVAL
2010

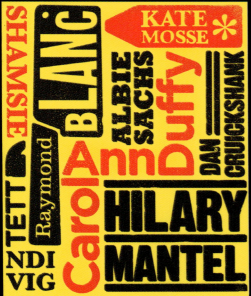

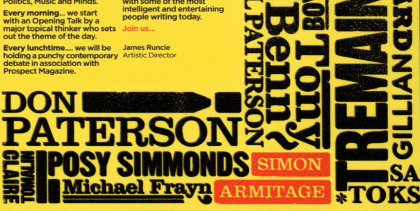

Welcome

A Book Festival is a meeting of minds; a shared opportunity to think about what it means to be alive; right here, right now.

This year each day has its own dedicated theme: anything from contemporary Britain to ancient Rome, Shakespeare, Politics, Music and Minds.

Every morning... we start with an Opening Talk by a major topical thinker who sets out the theme of the day.

Every lunchtime.... we will be holding a punchy contemporary debate in association with Prospect Magazine.

Every afternoon... there's History, Biography, and some of the most exciting voices in contemporary fiction.

And every evening... there's a performance of a play, a comedy or a reading together with a Face to Face interview with some of the most intelligent and entertaining people writing today.

Join us...

James Runcie
Artistic Director

Imagine:
UK

Project: Cake Liberation
Front Identity. Art
Director: David Caunce.
Designer: David Caunce.
Client: Caroline Turner.

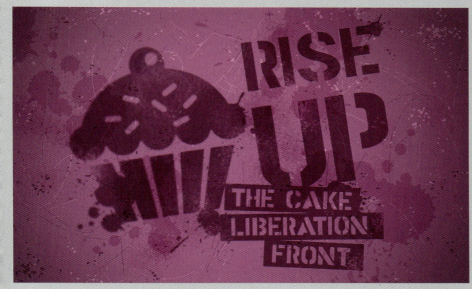

A closer look

Imagine:
UK

This identity for the Cake Liberation Front was created with a rather tongue-in-cheek proletariat protest movement vibe to it. It is kept very much alive with a campaign of messages that can be freely daubed onto posters and walls (using washable inks no doubt!).

Using a stencil font will always create a fairly military or militant feel to the project, but it's softened here with the use of more feminine colors.

THE CAKE LIBERATION FRONT

RISE UP

By spraying the graphics through stencils, the free-form nature of this work is really brought alive. Every piece becomes unique, and the erosion of the font along with overspill and blurring help make it a very powerful piece of free-form type.

Traditi onal:Type

Chapter 5

ype

New traditionalism:
Bethany Heck.

New
traditi
onalism.

The decision to use "vintage" typefaces, techniques, and aesthetics can come from a variety of motivations. Designers tend to be collectors and lovers of informational miscellany and minutiae, and vintage type is the perfect outlet to express those carnal desires in an effective and acceptable way.

Vintage designs are a celebration of their times, their economies, and their progress. They come loaded with history and meaning and tend to be obtuse in the way they go about their business. It is refreshing to look at design that has such a clear voice when you are searching for the right direction in your own work. There is a joy in historical design; A freedom to use a dozen typefaces in one design, the eccentricities of a typeface designed on the fly by a worker in a wood type factory, and the bold, straightforward language used to sell a bottle of soda are all cathartic to us now, free from the burdens we can feel when doing our own work. These pieces have a special sense of emotion, evoking places and moods on top of their visual aesthetics. Vintage designs have reminded designers to take risks, to mix more typefaces and break more rules.

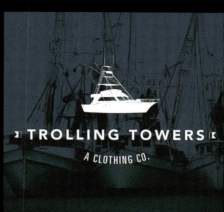

It's easier to separate yourself from historical design work than that of your peers. The technology standards and conventions were vastly different than they are now, and it enables you to look at the work objectively and closely study its formal attributes. The limitations of the time often forced unique solutions for dealing with type and composition. Now that we are separated from the context of those earlier works, we can look on them with our own set of tools, rules, and needs and reconfigure them in fresh ways that retain the charm of the original while fulfilling the needs of modern day. The gaudy, superfluous typefaces of the Victorian period can be given new life when put in a controlled setting, and the surprisingly complicated composition on a baseball ticket from the 1930s can be revived with careful typeface selections. The goal is not rote reproduction of vintage designs; it is to reimagine them in a new age.

The right selection of a historically inspired typeface can bring your work an extra layer of meaning and importance. Older designs have an added weight to them, an importance and meaning that goes beyond the formal aspects of the face that comes from decades of use and exposure. We can connect with a typeface without knowing why because it subliminally references the careful craft of a sign painter or the stylized geometric shapes of the Art Deco movement.

It's refreshing to look at a physical object for a spark instead of a computer screen. Seeing something physical that's still around decades after its creation is an inspiration in a multitude of ways. It's design out of its original context, free from comparisons of whatever trends were popular at the time, once again fresh and new. It's also a reminder of the importance and longevity of design. Design can be timeless, cherished, and treasured, and that's an exciting thing to remember. I think there is more to looking to past designs than just seeking a spark of visual stimulation. There is an element of reverence and respect tied to it as well. By resurrecting a design element from the past, you are honoring it and proving that it was a worthwhile endeavor in a way you hope your own work will be respected in the future.

Extra Credit Projects:
USA

Project: *Chow by the Tracks* P.O.P. poster campaign. Art Director: Joshua Best. Client: Choo Choo Grill.

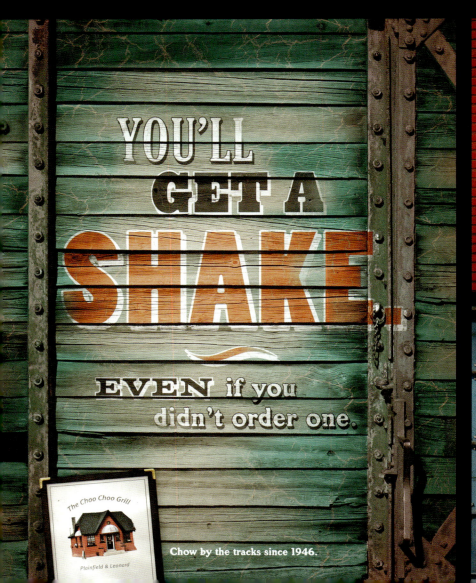

Fuszion:
USA

Project: The Georgetown
French Market. Art
Directors: Rick Heffner,
Greg Spraker. Designer:
Dan Delli-Colli. Client:
Georgetown (DC)
Business Improvement
District.

I Love Dust:
UK

Project: I Love Dust meat
packaging promo. Art
Directors: Mark Graham,
Ben Beach. Designer:
I Love Dust. Client: I Love
Dust.

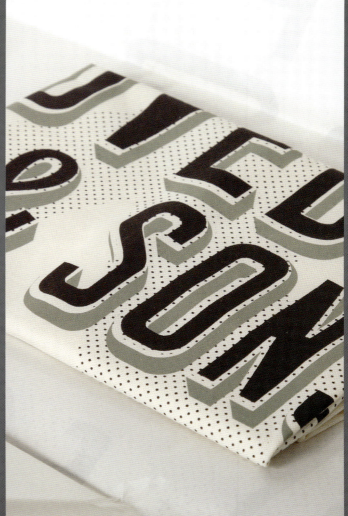

A closer look

I Love Dust:
UK

This retro–styled meat packaging was used by I Love Dust as the wrap for their choice cuts self–promotional brochure.

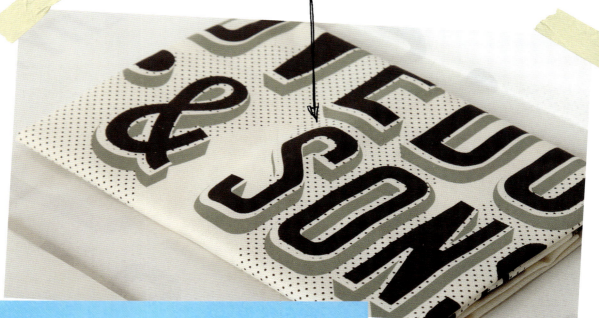

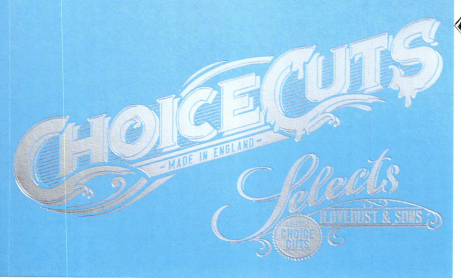

The brochure itself uses some very retro type styling and detail to great effect.

The type was created in—house and screen printed onto newsprint to add authenticity.

The typography is really detailed, right down to the sticker holding down the packaging.

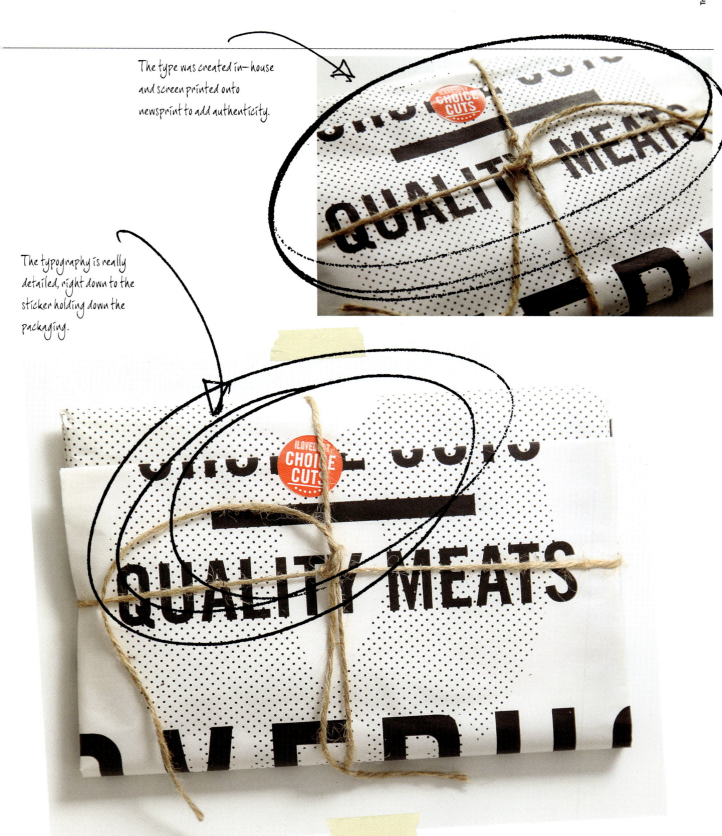

Burnthebook:
UK

Project: Burnthebook
branding, a design that
references traditional
bookbinding and
publishing marks.
Art Director: Simon
Duckworth. Designer:
Bobbie Haslett. Client:
Self-promotion.

Sensus Design
Factory Zagreb:
Croatia

Project: Dario Vlahovic
Architects, visual
identity. Art Director:
Nedjeljko Spoljar.
Designers: Nedjeljko
Spoljar, Kristina Spoljar.
Client: Dario Vlahovic
Architects.

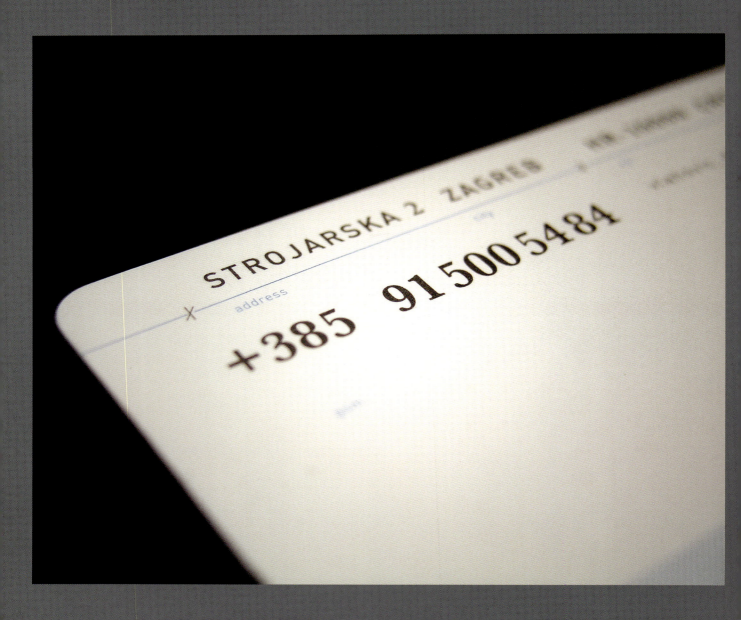

Project: Branding & identity,
collateral design and
restaurant signage for
French restaurant, Cocotte.
Art Director: Yah-Leng Yu.
Designer: Yah-Leng Yu.
Design & Craft Production:
Tianyu Isaiah Zheng.
Photography: Michael Tan
(Mika Images). Client:
Cocotte.

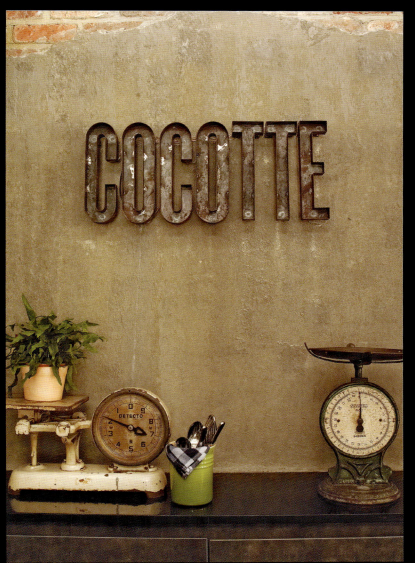

Thinkmule™:
USA

Project: Oddlings logo.
Designer: Thinkmule™.
Client: MOD Livin'.

Project: 13 Jolly Souls.
Designer: Thinkmule™.
Client: Illiterate Gallery.

Project: Spirits of 76.
Designer: Thinkmule™.
Client: Indy Ink.

Project: JibPig.
Designer: Thinkmule™.
Client: Thinkmule™.

Thinkmule™:
USA

Project: Jolly B 13 Cat.
Designer: Thinkmule™.
Client: Illiterate Gallery.

Project: Corporate
identity for Pauls
Schwester, a café in the
city of Cologne. The
owner of this café is (as
the german name
reveals) Pauls sister. Art
Director: Helge Rieder.
Designer: Helge Rieder.
Client: Pauls Schwester.

Sensus Design
Factory Zagreb:
Croatia

Project: Marc Chagall
monograph. Art Director:
Nedjeljko Spoljar.
Designers: Nedjeljko
Spoljar, Kristina Spoljar.
Client: Galerija Klovicevi
dvori.

Sensus Design
Factory Zagreb:
Croatia

Project: *The Best of*
catalogue. Art Director:
Nedjeljko Spoljar.
Designers: Nedjeljko
Spoljar, Kristina Spoljar.
Client: ArjoWiggins.

Sensus Design
Factory Zagreb:
Croatia

Project: *Post Scriptum*
catalogue. Art Director:
Nedjeljko Spoljar.
Designers: Nedjeljko
Spoljar, Kristina Spoljar.
Client: ArjoWiggins.

Voice:
Australia

Project: Estate range of wines. Art Directors: Anthony De Leo, Scott Carslake. Designer: Anthony De Leo. Client: Longview Vineyard.

Voice:
Australia

Project: Business
Stationery. Art Directors:
Anthony De Leo, Scott
Carslake. Designer:
Anthony De Leo. Client:
Longview Vineyard.

A closer look

Voice:
Australia

Longview is a stunning family owned Australian vineyard located in the Adelaide Hills. Set on undulating slopes reminiscent of classic old world estates, it has quickly established itself as one the most awarded vineyards in the region since its first vintage in 2001. Voice has reflected this mix of tradition and modernity in the branding of Longview Vineyard and its Estate range of wines.

Each product is unique, with its own typographic personality, but together the bottles create a broader personality for the range: unique and beautiful on their own, but tight-knit as a family of brands.

The "rule-breaking" type layout really gives the brand a modern edge, while the font itself keeps the sense of tradition required for wine labeling.

And there's a little bit of added type wit here as the name is also set in stacked form.

Even the simple cropping of the brand name helps give a little bit of typographic edge to the labeling.

Even the stationery cheekily crops off the vineyard's logo, reflecting the quirky styling of the entire brand.

How often is a client brave enough to allow the product name to be played with so much that legibility may be impaired. All credit to Voice and Longview for pushing the boundaries and giving us something more interesting to talk about at the dining table.

Sensus Design
Factory Zagreb:
Croatia

Project: *Zlatko Prica*
monograph. Art Director:
Nedjeljko Spoljar.
Designers: Nedjeljko
Spoljar, Kristina Spoljar.
Client: Kabinet grafike
HAZU.

Magma Brand Design:
Germany

Project: *Slanted
Magazine*. Art
Directors: Lars
Harmsen, Flo Gaertner.
Designer: Julia Kahl.
Client: *Slanted
Magazine*.

TYPE ESSAYS

—» P. 129

8

ES

SAYS

THE REVOLUTION WON'T BE SET IN GARAMOND
--- --------- ----- -- --- -- -------
Von Alex Negrelli

Die Schreibmaschine als politisches Instrument

Die Schreibmaschine nimmt in der Ikonografie politischer Bewegungen
eine besondere Rolle ein. Ihr markantes Schriftbild taucht immer wieder als Ausdruck
relevanter Texte auf und ist somit quasi Äußerung einer bestimmten Epoche

So wie sich heu
und so

SLANTED 11
THE
REVOLUTION
WON'T BE
SET IN
GARAMOND

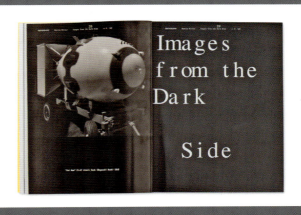

Images
from the
Dark

Side

Project: Voice brand
identity. Art Directors:
Anthony De Leo, Scott
Carslake. Client: Voice.

Q:
Germany

Burge Agency:
UK

Bethany Heck:
USA

Thinkmule™:
USA

Project: Eigenwillig logo
for a fashion label. Art
Directors: Matthias Frey,
Alexander Ginter. Client:
Eigenwillig.

Project: Silvåpünkt
branding. Designer:
Paul Burgess. Client:
Silverpoint.

Project: Gaslight District logo.
Designer: Bethany Heck.
Client: Self-initiated.

Project: Horn Thinkmule™.
Designer: Thinkmule™.
Client: Thinkmule™.

EIGENWILLIG

NORDIC OUTDOOR

Gaslight District

VICTORIAN INSPIRED CLOTHING

U.S.A

Ramp Creative:
USA

Project: Agostoni
chocolate packaging
and positioning.
Art Director: Michael
Stinson. Designer:
Tsz Chan. Client: ICAM
Cioccolato.

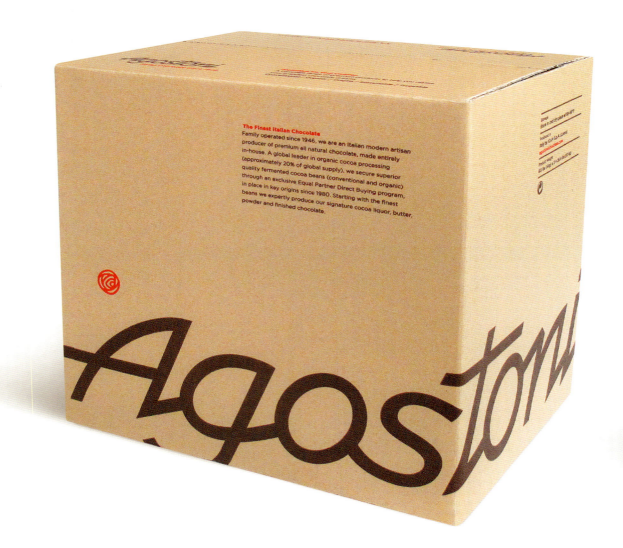

The Finest Italian Chocolate
Family operated since 1946, we are an Italian modern artisan
producer of premium all natural chocolate, made entirely
in-house. A global leader in organic cocoa processing
(approximately 20% of global supply), we secure superior
quality fermented cocoa beans (conventional and organic)
through an exclusive Equal Partner Direct Buying program,
in place in key origins since 1980. Starting with the finest
beans we expertly produce our signature cocoa liquor, butter,
powder and finished chocolate.

Project: Eephus League
Warm Up Sweater
poster. Designer:
Bethany Heck. Client:
Self-initiated.

Bethany Heck:
USA

Type: 219

Project: Packaging for
Eephus League
scorekeeping pencils
and buttons. Designer:
Bethany Heck. Client:
Self-initiated.

Bethany Heck:
USA

Project: Eephus League
Suicide Squeeze poster
and cigar box. Designer:
Bethany Heck. Client:
Self-initiated.

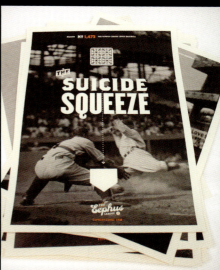

A closer look

Bethany Heck:
USA

Baseball has its own traditions, language, and rules and has remained relatively unchanged throughout its history, but new players, coaches, commentators, and fans pass through each day and add to its culture. Baseball is obsessed with record keeping. Every pitch, strike, and hit is recorded by hundreds of people each day. The Eephus League of Baseball Minutiae is an offshoot of the spirit of codification and history making. The Eephus League is also a tool for new fans to learn all of the many facets of the game, from scorekeeping to detailed statistics, and how to throw the perfect forkball.

The typography gives this project a really retro feel, but it also feels relevant today, especially with the rise in popularity of new traditionalism in design and the respect for heritage in branding.

The Eephus League posters use historically inspired typefaces in a bold way to complement photographs of turn-of-the-century ballplayers.

REASON N° 1,473 THE EEPHUS LEAGUE LOVES BASEBALL

THE
SUICIDE
SQUEEZE

THE Eephus LEAGUE

Heck has created a whole world of baseball that lives and breaths tradition through its photography, graphic detail, and above all, typography.

It would be unusual to use this kind of type styling on a modern, corporate business (although it would be great to see), but it's right at home here, reigniting the passion for baseball.

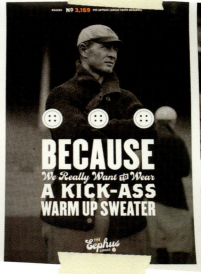

The packaging for the Eephus League baseball scorekeeping pencils and buttons uses paint cans, which can become keepsakes and are reusable.

Simon & Goetz Design:
Germany

Project: *221/222plus*, the customer magazine of the private bank Sal. Oppenheim jr. & Cie. Art Director: Bernd Vollmöller. Designers: Dörte Fischer, Bernd Vollmöller. Client: Sal. Oppenheim jr. & Cie.

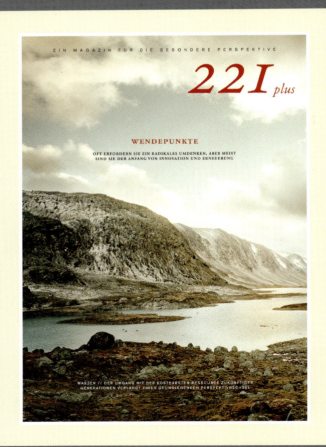

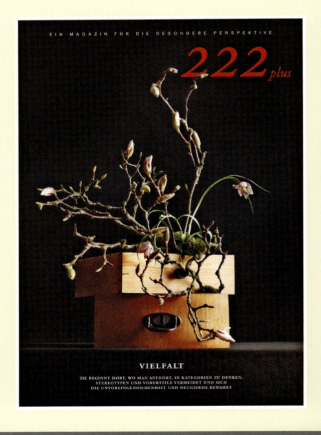

Sensus Design
Factory Zagreb:
Croatia

Project: *First Shot 2009*
posters. Art Director:
Nedjeljko Spoljar.
Designers: Nedjeljko
Spoljar, Kristina Spoljar.
Client: Galerija Klovicevi
dvori.

Bethany Heck:
USA

Project: Royal Theatre
letterpress poster.
Designer: Bethany Heck.
Client: Self-initiated.

Savannah College of Art and Design: USA

Project: Verticle composition using the word typography and numerals, focused on counterforms. Art Director: Professor Louis Baker. Designer: Adam Johnson. Client: Class Project.

Harcus Design:
Australia

Project: Y/Our Yalumba.
Each bottle sports two
different Ys, front and
back, silk-screened
onto the bottles. Art
Director: Annette
Harcus. Designer:
Annette Harcus.
Client: Yalumba.

Project: Logo redesign
for VFFF, a philanthropic
foundation established
by Sir Vincent and Lady
Fairfax to benefit and
care for the Australian
community with an
emphasis on nurturing
children and young
people. Art Director:
Annette Harcus.
Designer: Phoebe
Besley. Client: Vincent
Fairfax Family
Foundation.

Vincent Fairfax Family
Foundation

Sensus Design
Factory Zagreb:
Croatia

Project: Josip Klarica
monograph. Art Director:
Nedjeljko Spoljar.
Designers: Nedjeljko
Spoljar, Kristina Spoljar.
Client: Galerija Klovicevi
dvori.

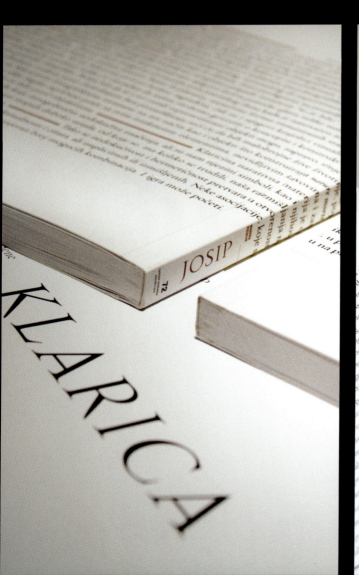

Sensus Design
Factory Zagreb:
Croatia

Project: Metalprint
mailing. Art Director:
Nedjeljko Spoljar.
Designers: Nedjeljko
Spoljar, Kristina Spoljar.
Client: Iggesund
Paperboard.

Felix Culpa Group:
USA

Project: NIU College of
Business 50 Year
Anniversary type
treatments. Designer:
Jason James Petersen.
Client: Nothern Illinois
University.

≈ NIU COLLEGE OF BUSINESS ≈

50 YEARS

Celebrating Our Past, Building Your Future

1961–2011

Bruketa & Žinić:
Croatia

Project: Incanto.
Creative Directors:
Miran Tomičić, Davor
Bruketa, Tonka Lujanac.
Art Director, Designer,
Copywriter: Tonka
Lujanac. Typographer:
Nicola Đurek. Client:
Fructus.

Bruketa & Žinić:
Croatia

Project: Galić wines,
packaging design based
on a stylized vine, in the
shape of the first letter of
the brand name. Creative
Directors: Davor
Bruketa, Nikola Žinić.
Art Director, Designer:
Sandra Bolfek. Bottle
Designer: Goga Golik.
Copywriter: Ivan Čadež.
Client: Galić.

Rashi Gandhi:
India

Project: Magazine
header. Art Director:
Rashi Ketan Gandhi.
Designer: Rashi Ketan
Gandhi. Client: *Glimpse
Zine*.

42ink Design:
Canada

Project: Hooked logo, for
a brand-new sustainable
seafood boutique. Art
Director: Kirstin Thomas.
Designer: Kirstin
Thomas. Client: Hooked.

State of Mind:
Greece

Project: State of Mind Art
Collective logo. Art
Director: Ryme63.
Designer: Ryme63.
Client: Self-promotional.

**Schellhas
Design:**
USA

Project: Skateboard
deck design. Art
Director: Hans Schellhas.
Designer: Hans
Schellhas. Client: Versus
Skateboards.

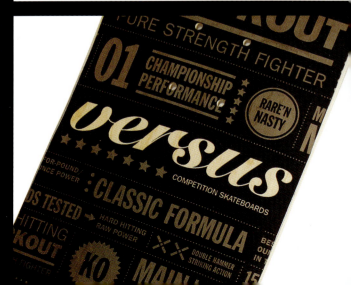

Simon & Goetz Design:
Germany

Project: *221/222plus*, a page from the customer magazine of the private bank Sal. Oppenheim jr. & Cie. Art Director: Bernd Vollmöller. Designers: Dörte Fischer, Bernd Vollmöller. Client: Sal. Oppenheim jr. & Cie.

One Lucky Guitar, Inc:
USA

Project: Promotional gig poster for Ike Reilly. Client: One Lucky Guitar, Inc.

EIN UNTERNEHMEN IST WIE EIN BIOTOP: BEIDE BRAUCHEN EIN AUSGEWOGENES GLEICHGEWICHT DIE HERAUSFORDERUNG BESTEHT DARIN, DIE RICHTIGE MISCHUNG ZU FINDEN UND INDIVIDUELLE VIELFALT ZU EINEM FUNKTIONIERENDEN GANZEN ZU VEREINEN.

HARD LUCK STORIES / Lyrics by Ike Reilly

the ballad of jack and haley ...

the reformed church of the assault rifle band ...

sheet metal moon ...

the golden corner ...

LUCKY TEN
PRESENTS

THE IKE REILLY ASSASSINATION

THE TIGER ROOM | SATURDAY, JULY 31

9PM | $6 | 21+ | WITH THE SACRED BRONCOS

TICKETS AT BROWNPAPERTICKETS.COM
IKEREILLY.NET | ONELUCKYGUITAR.COM/LUCKYTEN

Sensus Design
Factory Zagreb:
Croatia

Project: HUO AO Report.
Art Director: Nedjeljko
Spoljar. Designers:
Nedjeljko Spoljar,
Kristina Spoljar. Client:
Croatian Insurance
Bureau (HUO).

Project: Trolling Towers logo.
Designer: Bethany Heck.
Client: Trolling Towers.

Bethany Heck:
USA

Project: Title screen for EA
Sport's Two Steps From
Greatness, which focuses
on high school athletes.
Art Director: Larry Balutis.
Designer: Bethany Heck.
Client: EA Sports.

Sensus Design
Factory Zagreb:
Croatia

Project: *The 4th Croatian
Graphic Triennial*
catalog. Art Director:
Nedjeljko Spoljar.
Designers: Nedjeljko
Spoljar, Kristina Spoljar.
Client: Kabinet grafike
HAZU.

Project: The Arrogant
Butcher outdoor mural.
Art Directors: John
Johnson, Stewart West,
Jason Johnson.
Designer: Jason
Johnson. Client: Fox
Restaurant Concepts.

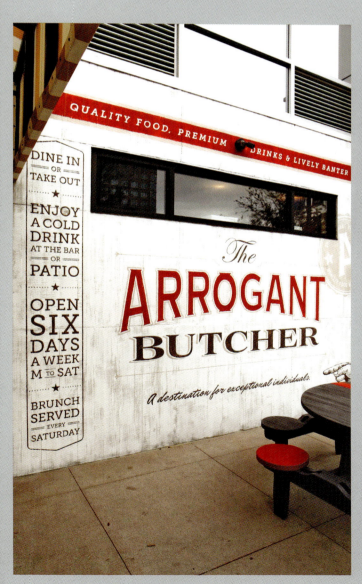

Sensus Design
Factory Zagreb:
Croatia

Project: *The 5th Croatian Graphic Triennial* catalog. Art Director: Nedjeljko Spoljar. Designers: Nedjeljko Spoljar, Kristina Spoljar. Client: Kabinet grafike HAZU.

Project: Leo Ingwer
Identity. Designers:
Megan Forb, Albert
Ignacio. Client: Leo
Ingwer.

Bethany Heck:
USA

Project: A poster
for an AIGA event
honoring Lon Doffsen.
Client: Self-initiated.

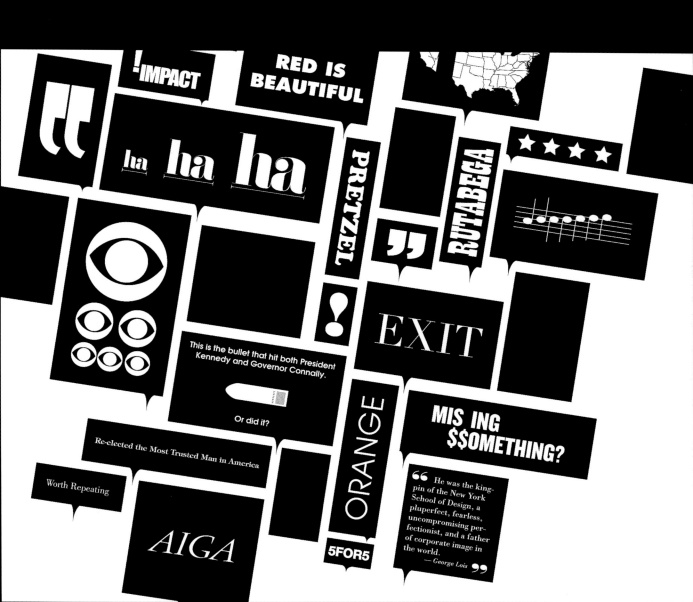

Foreign Policy
Design Group:
Singapore

Project: The Roof
restaurant branding,
identity and menu
design. Art Directors:
Yah-Leng Yu, Arthur
Chin. Designer: Tianyu
Isaiah Zheng. Client: The
Waterhouse at South
Bund, Shanghai.

Dorian:
Spain

Project: Commemorative wines for the cultural event "La Rioja Tierra Abierta, La Fiesta Barroca 2011". Art Director: Dorian. Designer: Dorian. Client: Palacios Remondo.

etcorporate design:
Germany

Project: Corporate design
for Baby Ansorge. Art
Directors: Elisa Huber,
Anton Huber. Designers:
Elisa Huber, Anton Huber.
Client: Baby Ansorge.

sparc, inc:
USA

Project: Identity for a
lingerie and sportswear
boutique owned by
Priscilla. The nickname's
two Ls make a P. Art
Director: Richard Cassis.
Designer: Richard Cassis.
Client: scilla Boutique.

Becky Ford:
Spain

Project: Identity for a
Spanish Dance School.
Art Director: Becky Ford.
Designer: Becky Ford.
Client: Castellano School
of Dance.

Voice:
Australia

Project: Packaging and
branding for The Store.
Art Directors: Anthony De
Leo, Scott Carslake.
Designer: Tom Crosby.
Client: The Store.

Project: Hannah, nursery
artwork. Art Director:
Darren Bodnaruk.
Designer: Darren
Bodnaruk.

May23.2010

Design
Hoch Drei:
Germany

Project: Hand-drawn
artwork for Daimler
Sustainability Report
article "360 Degrees".
Art Directors: Wolfram
Schaffer, Isabell Zirbeck.
Designer: Ioannis
Karanasios. Client:
Daimler AG.

Danny Warner
Design:
USA

Project: "Ligatura
Schematica" for
forthcoming experimental
image-novel. Art Director:
Danny Warner. Designer:
Danny Warner. Client:
Steve Tomasula (fiction
writer).

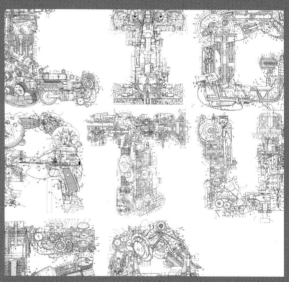

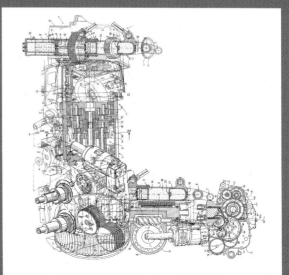

Sensus Design
Factory Zagreb:
Croatia

Project: Werner Bischof
Photographs. Art
Director: Nedjeljko
Spoljar. Designers:
Nedjeljko Spoljar,
Kristina Spoljar. Client:
Galerija Klovicevi dvori.

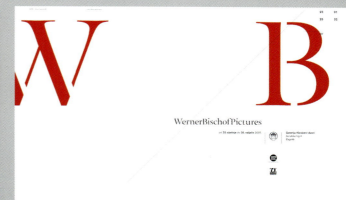

Sensus Design
Factory Zagreb:
Croatia

Project: *Conqueror
Catalog 4.0.* Art Director:
Nedjeljko Spoljar.
Designers: Nedjeljko
Spoljar, Kristina Spoljar.
Client: ArjoWiggins.

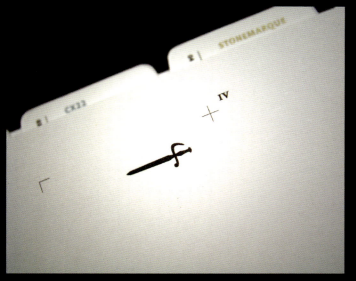

Foreign Policy
Design Group:
Singapore

Project: Table N°1,
Shanghai, branding,
identity and collateral
design. Art Directors:
Yah-Leng Yu, Arthur Chin.
Designer: Tianyu Isaiah
Zheng. Client: Table N°1,
Shanghai.

Bruketa & Žinić:
Croatia

Project: *The Book of
Genesis*. Creative
Directors, Copywriters,
Art Directors: Davor
Bruketa, Nikola Žinić.
Art Director, Designer:
Tomislav Jurica Kaćunić.
Copywriters: Ivan Čadež,
Daniel Vuković. Client:
Abus (Hladno pivo).

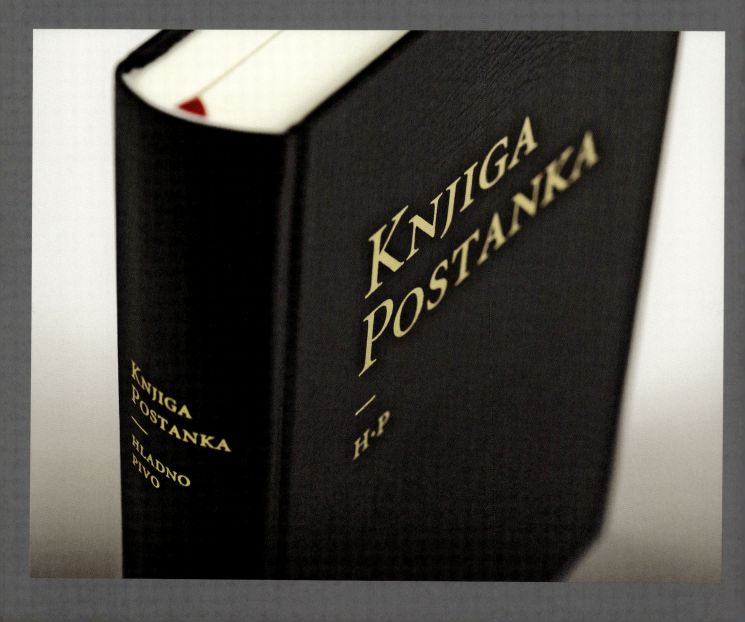

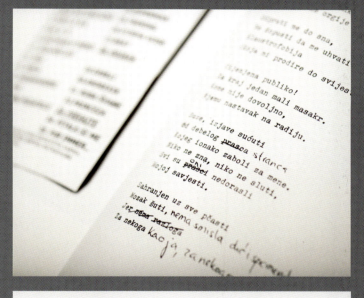

Project: Devil's Elbow
Magnum. Art Directors:
Anthony De Leo, Scott
Carslake. Designer:
Anthony De Leo. Client:
Longview Vineyard.

Voice:
Australia

Project: Blends. Art
Directors: Anthony De
Leo, Scott Carslake.
Designers: Anthony De
Leo, Scott Carslake.
Client: Longview
Vineyard.

Voice:
Australia

Project: Yakka Magnum.
Art Directors: Anthony De
Leo, Scott Carslake.
Designer: Anthony De
Leo. Client: Longview
Vineyard.

Voice:
Australia

Project: W. Wagtail.
Art Directors: Anthony De
Leo, Scott Carslake.
Designer: Shane Keane.
Client: Longview
Vineyard.

Project: *Waitrose*
magazine. Art Directors:
Ben Beach, Mark
Graham. Designer:
I Love Dust. Client:
Waitrose.

Project: VH1 Letterpress
Lyrics. Art Directors:
Mark Graham, Ben
Beach. Designer: I Love
Dust. Client: VH1.

BoRN DOWN IN A DEAD MANS TOWN THE FIRST KICK I TOOK
WAS WHEN I HIT THE GROUND YOU END UP LIKE A DOG
THATS BEEN BEAT TOO MUCH
TILL YOU SPEND HALF YOUR LIFE JUST COVERING UP
GOT IN A LITTLE HOMETOWN JAM, SO THEY PUT A RIFLE IN MY HAND
SENT ME OFF I WAS BORN IN THE SAID SON IF
TO A FOREIGN LAND IT WAS UP TO ME
TO GO AND KILL USA WENT DOWN TO SEE
THE YELLOW MAN MY V.A. MAN
HE SAID SON,
DONT YOU UNDERSTAND
I HAD A BROTHER AT KHE SAHN
FIGHTING OFF THE VIET CONG THEYRE STILL THERE, HES ALL GONE
HE HAD A WOMAN HE LOVED IN SAIGON
I GOT A PICTURE OF HIM IN HER ARMS NOW
DOWN IN THE SHADOW OF THE PENITENTIARY
OUT BY THE GAS FIRES OF THE REFINERY
IM TEN YEARS BURNING
DOWN THE
ROAD

COME
BACK
HOME
TO THE
REF
INER Y
HIRING MAN

NOWHERE TO RUN
AINT GOT
NOWHERE
TO GO

Project: Branding for
Island Creek Oyster Bar.
Art Director: Jennifer
Lucey-Brzoza. Designer:
Jennifer Lucey-Brzoza.
Client: Island Creek
Oyster Bar.

ICOB

MADE IN

DUXBURY MA

ISLAND CREEK

OYSTER

BAR

№ CCB45 MA

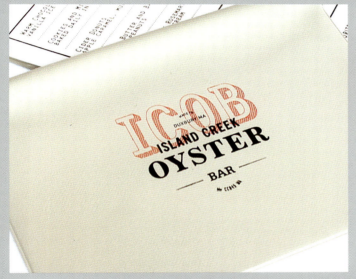

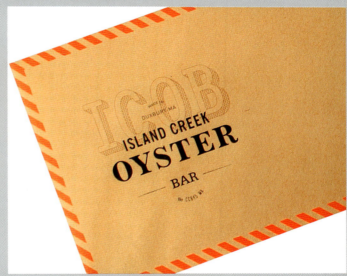

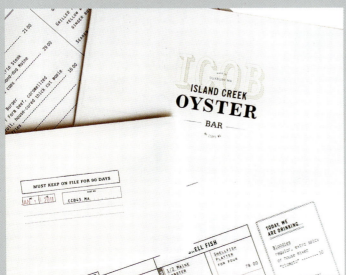

Love Dust:
UK

Project: Love Your Bike
promotional event
posters. Art Directors:
Ben Beach, Mark
Graham. Designer:
Love Dust. Client:
Portsmouth City Council,
Portsmouth University.

LOVE YOUR BIKE
Portsmouth
30.05.10

· LOVE YOUR BIKE ·

Sunday 30th May 2010
Southsea, Portsmouth

love/design/build/fix/create/modify/recyele/customise

A free event open to all ages.
Sponsored by University of Portsmouth / Portsmouth City Council.

Southsea Skatepark / 10 am 'til 5pm
Southsea Common, Clarence Esplanade, Southsea, PO5 3NZ

Ian Parmiter's Antiques / DJ & Vintage Bike Showcase from 4pm
2 Exmouth Road, Southsea, PO5 2QL

Little Johnny Russell's / 6pm 'till late - Free food
12 Albert Road, Southsea, PO5 2SH

Bike culture is an important part of cycling and regaining the streets.
This event aims to encourage participants to fully embrace the possibilities of
connecting with their bikes and explore the many ways that they can improve
it's appearance and design. The event will feature Workshops, Bike Demo's,
Bike Polo, Marketstalls, Bike Artwork, Bike Safety and a Showcase Bike Arena.

Get involved e-mail: claire.sambrook@port.ac.uk or call on 07843 057897

WWW.LOVEYOURBIKEPORTSMOUTH.CO.UK

In collaboration with: University of Portsmouth, Ian Parmiter, Strong Island, Bored of Southsea, Portsmouth City Council, ilovedust, Portsmouth Cycle Forum, Healthy Towns Initiative, Women Who Cycle, Southsea Fixed Gear Fight Club, Ben Wilson, Cargo Bullitt Bikes, Wishbone NZ Bikes, Raw Bamboo Bikes, Benedict Radcliffe, Tokyo Fixed Gear, Hemingway Design, Portsmouth Creative Movement, Viaggio Velo, Bike Off, Creative Campus Initiative, Hokey Spokes UK, Nova Industries, Cycleworks, Cycloc, Respect Programme, Hampshire Constabulary and GoCycle.

LOVE YOUR BIKE
Portsmouth
30.05.10

Bethany Heck:
USA

Project: A map
examining the retail
layout of Grafton Street
in Dublin, Ireland.
Designer: Bethany Heck.

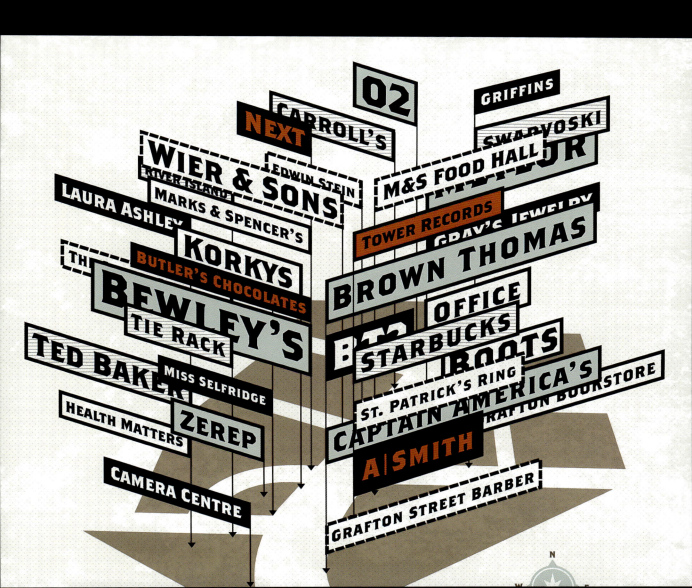

Contributor:Index

Contributor Index.

344 Design, LLC
344design.com

42ink Design
42ink.com

804© GRAPHIC DESIGN
achtnullvier.com

Alex Trochut
alextrochut.com

Aloof
aloofdesign.com

And Partners
andpartnersny.com

Another Limited Rebellion
alrdesign.com

Artiva Design
artiva.it

Becky Ford
becky-ford.com

Bethany Heck
heckhouse.com

Blok Design
blokdesign.com

Bowling Green State Univeristy, School of Art Graphic Design Division
art.bgsu.edu

Brigada
bruketa-zinic.com

Bruketa & Žinić
bruketa-zinic.com

Burge Agency
burgeagency.com

Burnthebook
burnthebook.co.uk

Curious
curiouslondon.com

Danny Warner Design
danny-warner.com

Design Hoch Drei
design-hoch-drei.de

D-Fuse
dfuse.com

Dorian
estudiodorian.com

DRNBDNRK
twitter.com/DRNBDNRK

Elliott Burford
elliottburford.com

etcorporate design
etcorporate.com

Extra Black: Graphic Design Studio
extrablack.ws

Extra Credit Projects
extracreditprojects.com

Felix Culpa Group
felixculpagroup.com

Foreign Policy Design Group
foreignpolicydesign.com

Fuszion
fuszion.com

Sophia Georgopoulou
sophiag.com

Go Welsh
gowelsh.com

Harcus Design
harcus.com.au

I Love Dust
ilovedust.com

Imagine
imagine-cga.co.uk

Jay Roeder
jayroeder.com

Jillian Coorey
jilliancoorey.com

Jimmy Ball Design
jimmyball.com

Joe Miller's Company
joemillersco.com

Jose Palma Visual Works
josepalma.com

Juicebox Designs
juiceboxdesigns.com

Ken-Tsai Lee Image Design Company
behance.net/kentsailee

**Kiku Obata &
Company**
kikuobata.com

LSDspace
lsdspace.com

**Magma Brand
Design**
magmabranddesign.de

**Michael
Lashford Design**
michaellashford.com

Tony Seddon
tonyseddon.com

Oat
oatcreative.com

**One Lucky
Guitar, Inc.**
oneluckyguitar.com

**One Man's
Studio**
onemansstudio.com

Peter Ladd
peterladd.com

**Petralito Rotiroti
Associati**
pr-a.it

Q
q-home.de

Marshall Rake
marshallrake.com

Ramp Creative
rampcreative.com

Rashi Gandhi
rashigandhi.com

Rose
rosedesign.co.uk

Shawn Sanem
ssanem.com

**Savannah
College of Art
and Design**
scad.edu

Schellhas Design
behance.net/schellhas

**Scorsone/
Drueding**
sdposters.com

**Sensus Design
Factory Zagreb**
sensusdesignfactory.com

**Silver Lining
Design**
silverlining-designs.com

**Simon & Goetz
Design**
simongoetz.de

**Sophy Lee
Design**
sophylee.com

sparc, inc
sparcinc.com

State of Mind
stateofminddesign.com

**Steers McGillan
Eves Design**
steersmcgillaneves.co.uk

Stephan Walter
stephanwalter.ch

Ten Gun Design
tengundesign.com

The Allotment
theallotmentbranddesign.com

**The Room
Design Studio**
theroom.com.au

Thinkmule™
thinkmule.com

**Thompson
Brand Partners**
thompsonbrandpartners.com

Thonik
thonik.nl

TunnelBravo
tunnelbravo.com

Un Mundo Feliz
unmundofeliz2.blogspot.com

Unfolding Terrain
unfoldingterrain.com

Uretsky & Co.
uretsky.net

Vamadesign
vamadesign.com

**VISUALMENTAL
STIMULI**
visualmentalstimuli.com

Viviana Gomez
vivianagomez.com

Voice
voicedesign.net

Wonksite Studio
wonksite.com

WORKtoDATE
worktodate.com

About the author:
Paul Burgess.

ut
e author.

Based in the UK, Paul Burgess has spent the last 20 years as creative director at some of London's fastest growing agencies and was creative director and partner at the iconic agency, Loewy.

He recently set up Burge Agency, which has a multi-disciplined approach to design, typography, and creative campaigns, working for some of the world's largest brands, as well as some of the smallest.

Paul has authored five other books including *1000 Type Treatments*.

THE LIBRARY
NEW COLLEGE
SWINDON